A collection of vision encounters

Douglas Tews

Encounters with Jesus

© 2018 by Douglas Tews

All rights reserved. No part of this publication may be reproduced, stored in a retrieval system, or transmitted in any form or by any means — electronic, mechanical, photocopying, recording or otherwise — without the prior written permission of the author.

Unless otherwise indicated, scripture quotations taken from The Holy Bible, New International Version® NIV®

Copyright © 1973, 1978, 1984, 2011 by Biblica, Inc.®

Used by permission. All rights reserved worldwide.

ISBN 978-1981138814

Cover Design by Douglas Tews
Image of Jesus by Del Parson from his painting:
"In His Glory" — Used with permission.

Endorsements

Doug Tews' incredible book, *Encounters with Jesus*, will help you proceed along your journey for more of the supernatural. It helps capture the very essence of the Lord Himself and will give you understanding and insight on what it's like to connect with Jesus, clearly hear His voice, and see what He is doing. Doug's reflections about his experiences are captivating and wonderful for instruction – and encourage you to seek your own face-to-face encounters with Jesus.

Encounters with Jesus has made a profound impact on my life. It is a powerful resource to help me easily enter into His presence. It has ignited a desire, a new passion, for more of the Lord – to seek His face like never before.
Make this book a part of your daily time with Lord and I promise – you will never be the same!

— Rev. Gary Oates
Author, *Open My Eyes, Lord*

It was a blessing to be with Doug when he started to experience these incredible visions of Jesus and we encouraged him to write them down so others could be blessed. While here on the Isle of Wight, Doug shared these with people in our meetings and every time blessing ensued.

I know this book will encourage your faith and thrill your heart as you immerse yourself and read through these powerful encounters!

— Christopher Cass
Founder, Revival Fire Ministries
Isle of Wight, United Kingdom

In *Encounters with Jesus*, Doug Tews has passionately pursued the world of the Spirit. He has learned to use the eyes and ears of his heart, even as Jesus did. These heavenly encounters are available to us all. I believe this book will inspire you to go further and deeper into the world of the Spirit. Be challenged! Be thrilled! Be inspired!

Thank you, Doug for this immeasurable gift to the body of Christ.

— Dr. Mark Virkler
Author, *4 Keys to Hearing God's Voice*

While reading through Doug's visions, I began to see Jesus as a gentle, benevolent, loving personhood of the Godhead. Doug's work has helped bring this closer to reality in my life.

Coming from a religious background where God was conveyed as angry and authoritarian, I grew up with the idea I had to earn merit to be accepted by God. My life as a believer taught me intellectually otherwise. However, this head knowledge wasn't sinking into my heart. When reading Doug's work, the Lord's anointing on his visions became apparent to me. They took me to a place of intimacy where Jesus, as He really is, became a greater reality to me.

While reading this material, I was beset by illness, a car accident, and the separation of my marriage. The reality of the character of Jesus conveyed through Doug's work empowered me to face and dispel the anxiety and depression I was experiencing. This is a real development in my life. I am grateful to God for blessing me with this book "for such a time as this." (Esther 4:14)

— Richard Helmbrecht
M.S. Psychology, BCaBA

This book left me with a sense of wanting. Wanting to know Jesus on this distinctly personal level. Doug Tews shows what its truly like to have Jesus as your Lord and friend at the same time. Lovely read!

— Erik Dattwyler
Web Page Designer, Coder

CONTENTS:

How It All Started 1
The First in A Series of Visual Experiences 9
Visiting the Sea of Galilee and Being Fed by Jesus 11
Jesus Loves Us in Simple Ways Too 13
Revisiting Galilee — Jesus Provides Some Very Special Bread 15
An Invitation 19
Allowing Jesus to Form Us 21
Jesus in Me! 23
A Lesson in The Ways of the Spirit 27
The Way of Man Versus the Way of God 31
The Woodland Garden 35
God Provides What We Need at This Moment 39
The Passage of Time: Our Perspective Versus God's 41
An Unexpected Encounter: We Have Friends We Don't Know About 45
Whoever Believes in Me Will Do the Works I Have Been Doing ... 51
The Choice Is Ours 55
A Lesson in God's Provision 57
"Follow Me" 61
The Tour Begins 65
Through The Door... Into Another Realm 71
An Invitation 79
An Opportunity Seemingly Lost 81
A Frank Talk with Jesus— In an Unexpected Place 83
Jesus Versus the Enemy — No Contest! 87
My First Visit into The Throne Room 89
A Lesson in God's Personality 93
Light Dispelling the Darkness 97
An Encounter with The Father 101
Preparing for an Encounter 105
An Encounter with The Holy Spirit 109

A Christmas Present from Jesus	115
Part Two: The Adventure Continues	117
Trusting in Jesus Casts Out All Fear	119
A Visit to A Fiery Place	125
Increasing Beauty	133
Another Missed Opportunity	137
"I Just Want You to Be with Me"	141
Root Pruning	143
An Unexpected Person Encourages Me: Trust in Jesus	147
Impeding the Flow of the Spirit	151
Joining Together with Jesus	153
Jesus Our Protector	155
Preparation for A Feast	157
The Impact of the Cross	161
The Fire of Purity	165
The Unveiling	169
Defeating the Storms	175
Confessing a Struggle	179
A Painful Lesson	183
"Everything I Make Is Pretty"	189
God's Infinite Perception	199
"I Give Abundantly"	205
"You Cannot Ask Too Much"	209
The Big Fish	211
"You Are Clean"	217
The Time of Preparation	223
A Heart for The Lost	227
Conclusions from This Journey So Far	233
The Most Important Key to	235
Entering and Experiencing the Spiritual Realm	235
Suggested Reading	243
About the Author	245

How It All Started

This was not my idea.

A few years ago, when I started having vision encounters with the Lord, I never dreamt of collecting and printing them for others to see. Originally, they were a part of my personal journal. I was simply pursuing the Lord, desiring to draw closer to Him in any way He might bless, through any doors He might open.

As these experiences unfolded, I had opportunity to share some of them with friends in a couple small groups. People were often touched by hearing them, in some instances significantly. One pastor friend observed this and suggested putting these experiences together in a book for easy sharing.

Initially I was resistant to this. I am not a self-promoting type of person and wouldn't want such a collection misconstrued in anyway. Rather, I was simply pursuing the Lord and these experiences happened. Not only have they born considerable fruit in my life, but seeing others repeatedly touched when hearing them gave me pause to reconsider.

What follows within these pages is an adventure. It is a story of seeking and pursuing the Lord. It is a story with both successes…and some personal failures.

How it began…

In 2010, I attended a conference in Exeter, England with guest speaker, Rev. Gary Oates. His book, "Open My Eyes, Lord" was…well, I guess you could say—a real eye opener! Although Gary shares some amazing encounters he's had with the Lord, those encounters are not the real focus of the book or teachings.

Rather, the book's emphasis is on developing an intimate relationship with the Lord. It seems many today are seeking experiences, gifts, or wonders. However, as Gary rightly points out, such things are not to be our primary focus. Our singular, most important pursuit must be to seek an intimate relationship with God. Everything else flows naturally out of that.

My spirit was quickened when I heard this. Witnessing many "doctrinal fads" in the church over the years left me discouraged. People would buy into this or that... often getting hurt and disillusioned. I knew in my spirit, priorities in some Christian circles were not in the best of order. It was refreshing to hear someone emphasize the need to FIRST establish a totally uncompromised, intimate relationship with God. It's not a quick fix. It takes work and dedication. But "things" people often seek, like miracles and wonders flow naturally out of that relationship. Conversely, when people seek spiritual phenomena without first establishing an intimate relationship with God, the phenomena often become the focus, invariably leading to imbalance and all sorts of problems.

Open My Eyes, Lord...

During one part of the conference, Gary shared a prayer of impartation over the group. He also provided numerous Biblical examples showing how people in the Bible saw and heard from the Lord. While at that conference, I had my first visual experience. It was short, but I saw a pillar of fire and the Lord spoke some very encouraging words to me.

During the next couple years, I had opportunity to enjoy further teaching and experienced a few more short, visual encounters, each time receiving fresh encouragement from the Lord. However, for some reason this didn't seem to flow over into my personal prayer life, despite my desire to experience the Lord in more intimate ways. As it happened, that was about to change early in the following year.

Getting me still...

In my desire to draw closer to the Lord, I purposely set out to seek Him where He was working in overt, powerful ways. During 2011 and 2012, I went on two mission trips with Gary Oates to South America and saw many amazing miracles... some of which were answers to my own prayers when praying for people.

As 2013 approached, I was looking forward to another mission trip that year. However, at the end of 2012, those plans were utterly dashed. Circumstances evolved forcing me to move from the apartment I was renting and finding a new home.

The place I had been living in for eight years was fully furnished. However, the new place was totally empty. Moving into and furnishing a new apartment—even with used items— was costly for someone with limited finances. The economic recession left me working only part time and with no savings. I had no choice but to put the expenses on my credit card knowing it would take about a year to pay off. My heart sank as I realized I couldn't afford to go anywhere during 2013, short of a financial miracle. In fact, I couldn't afford to go on any vacation period...not even a weekend away.

Realizing I would be stuck at home for a whole year, I had a decision to make. I could mope about and feel sorry for myself like the Israelites did in the desert—but what good did that accomplish? Or, I could look forward positively and trust the Lord had something planned for me at home. I chose the latter.

It turned out; keeping me in place without the distraction of upcoming trips was exactly what the Lord wanted. It created an extended period of uninterrupted time required for what He was about to do.

How to Hear God's Voice...

During a conference, I picked up a book by Mark Virkler that Gary Oates highly recommended. "How to Hear God's Voice" is large book of about 300 pages. It is, in fact, a comprehensive course Mark Virkler and his wife Patti have been teaching worldwide for many years.

This book acted like an "ignition key" for my subsequent experiences. Hungry and desirous for a deeper relationship with the Lord, I spent a number of weeks digesting the teachings within...and then putting them into practice as I lay myself before God.

Mark deals extensively with issues such as:

- Learning to quiet ourselves before the Lord (many today find this challenging).
- Eliminating idols in our hearts and focusing exclusively on Jesus.
- Testing and distinguishing between our thoughts, God's thoughts and those planted in our mind from the enemy.
- The value and need to record our experiences.
- The necessity of having mature, spiritual advisors who can come alongside, pray over, discern our experiences and help confirm what is of the Lord.

Mark also addresses many related issues in the Christian life, including a detailed examination of the many facets of prayer. He deals forthrightly with and clearly differentiates between Biblical prayer, meditation and experience versus "new age" counterfeits.

What these experiences are… and what they are not…

When reading through some of these encounters with the Lord, one might wonder whether they were "out of the body" experiences. To that I would answer, definitely not. I was always cognizant of where I physically was. However, these experiences were more impactful than if I was just relaxing and watching television. Rather, they were interactive, three dimensional, where I was seeing, hearing, feeling, tasting…and even smelling things in the spirit. I would best describe it as almost being in two places at once. I was totally cognizant of my physical surroundings, yet at the same time having experiences completely separate from that.

Was I seeing real places, or was I simply experiencing images painted on the screen of my mind by the Holy Spirit? I suspect some of both. When reading the experiences of Daniel, Ezekiel and John, it appears there were times they saw literal places. However, at other times what they witnessed seemed abstract, or allegorical in nature. Perhaps in those situations, they were witnessing something "painted" by the Holy Spirit on the screen of their minds to communicate truth.

The bottom line is, we really don't know…and it doesn't matter either. God is highly creative in the way He communicates and can do so in whatever manner He pleases. The final impact and truth being communicated to the hearer is what really matters. Hearing God speak changes people!

About the format...

In Mark's book, he discusses keeping a journal of one's experiences. For recording his own experiences, he would sit with his laptop, eyes closed and simply type as things unfolded before him. Because I can also touch-type (i.e., it's not necessary to see the keyboard) I realized I could do the same thing.

I learned to recognize when a vision was coming. Typically, I would get glimpses of something in my mind that would spontaneously recur throughout the day. In the evening, I would quiet myself before the Lord and ask what He would like to show me. As things unfolded before me, I tried to write down everything as best I could while they happened.

However, sometimes things happened at a speed where details didn't get completely recorded. Likewise, I might see something, but not fully understand it at the moment. I therefore found it valuable to write a separate "reflections afterwards" section to these narratives. The reflections section, as the name implies, contains reflections from my pondering regarding what I had just seen. It also provided the opportunity to fill in details I neglected to record as the experience occurred.

I soon realized the "reflections" section was often as important as the experience itself. Frequently, the Lord would continue to reveal things as I pondered the experience. In some cases, I would add further notes to the reflections months after the original experience, as subsequent revelation and understanding came to me.

Suggestions for reading this material...

This book is a series of adventures presented in chronological order. Therefore, if a reader were to skip about from one chapter to another, some things might not be understood. Many of these encounters stand well on their own. However, others have references to earlier experiences providing helpful context for understanding. Therefore, when reading these for the first time, it is advantageous to take them in order.

As a collection of individual experiences, it is also beneficial to pause and reflect after each. Attempting to read this book through in one or two sittings is not likely to be very edifying. I would suggest reading and meditating on only a few at a time. It's possible the Lord might choose to speak to you through some of these...or possibly even transport you into an encounter of your own!

In the beginning, the encounters were short and simple. However, over time they become lengthier, deeper, and in some cases more mysterious — at least when initially experienced. Like parables and visions experienced by others, the Lord seems to deliberately design these to be pondered.

Why share these?

Sharing always entails a certain risk as we allow ourselves to be vulnerable to others. Occasionally, some fairly personal, private thoughts are contained with this material. After all, this was never written with public consumption in mind. In most instances, I've allowed my inner thoughts to remain for others to see. As my personal struggles are revealed, so is God's overwhelming goodness and care. Others have frequently told me they benefitted from hearing or reading these and that's why they are being shared.

Over time, the Lord has addressed a few very private matters I elected not to share. However, what follows represents about 95% of what I experienced, up to the time this book was compiled.

Also, according to Mark Virkler's wise admonition, these writings have been shared with other mature Christians for the purpose of discernment.

The most important thing is this... The Lord wants to speak to every one of us. I'm no different from anybody else. If I can hear God speak and have encounters with Him, anybody can.

Therefore, I hope this encourages others to seek and encounter the Lord with all their heart, soul and mind.

—Douglas Tews

The First in A Series of Visual Experiences

In Mark Virkler's book, he occasionally presents a selection of scriptures to ponder. The idea is to meditate on the passages and see if the Spirit would draw me to any of them. If I felt drawn to a certain scripture, I would ask the Lord what He might like to show me. I would then wait and see what kind of pictures are revealed in my mind...

Revelation 22:1-2 (NIV)
Then the angel showed me the river of the water of life, as clear as crystal, flowing from the throne of God and of the Lamb down the middle of the great street of the city. On each side of the river stood the tree of life, bearing twelve crops of fruit, yielding its fruit every month. And the leaves of the tree are for the healing of the nations.

Psalm 1:2-3 (NIV)
² but whose delight is in the law of the LORD, and who meditates on his law day and night.
³ That person is like a tree planted by streams of water, which yields its fruit in season and whose leaf does not wither whatever they do prospers.

In my mind's eye, I saw the tree of life. I did not notice fruit, but saw the leaves. For healing? I want that. I plucked a few and rubbed them in my hands, crushing them also in my palms. That seemed to release something. I buried my face into my palms and leaves. The smell is aromatic and similar to eucalyptus. The presence of God's Spirit and peace enveloped me. I then felt I should eat one. It was placed within my mouth, but stuck to my tongue and wouldn't go down. I scraped at it and even turned it over, but it still wouldn't go down. I finally began to chew it, and then suddenly, whoosh, it went down of its own accord without me having to swallow. I'm trying another one, but the same thing has happened. It wants to stick to my tongue. Strange. I don't seem to be going any further. I'll have to come back to this and see what the Lord might be trying to show me.

I also sensed the water from the river was in the leaves, that's where the power came from. The leaves derive their life from the water of life...

John 15:4 8 (NIV)
⁴ Remain in me, as I also remain in you. No branch can bear fruit by itself; it must remain in the vine. Neither can you bear fruit unless you remain in me.
⁵ I am the vine; you are the branches. If you remain in me and I in you, you will bear much fruit; apart from me you can do nothing. ⁶ If you do not remain in me, you are like a branch that is thrown away and withers; such branches are picked up, thrown into the fire and burned. ⁷ If you remain in me and my words remain in you, ask whatever you wish, and it will be done for you. ⁸ This is to my Father's glory, that you bear much fruit, showing yourselves to be my disciples.

The source of everything is from the Spirit. He is within me. I must learn to recognize Him, learn to sense Him, learn to flow with Him. How do I learn?
"By spending time with Me." (the Lord)

Visiting the Sea of Galilee and Being Fed by Jesus

I felt led to read John's account of feeding the five thousand. "Lord, what would you like to say to me about this story?"

I'm sitting on the grassy slope above the lake. I'm in the midst of throngs of people. It's a sunny day. Pleasant. There are lots of voices around me. I hear a noise behind me and it's a tall, well-dressed man with a dark, bushy beard and something like a turban on his head. He sits down behind me. I have a sense he is an angel in the crowd... and sense there are other angels mingled about in the crowd as well. I sit waiting. Jesus is down there somewhere, but I can't see him. There seem to be people in the way of my vision. I stand up and look... I think I see Jesus, but he's so far away.

Suddenly, He's there right in front of me, his arms open wide. "Come I will feed you too. But I have much to offer you that is not of this world. The food that I offer is of the Spirit."

"Lord, I think I'm ready to eat something... at least I think I am."

"Come closer." I come closer to Jesus and kneel before him. My mouth opens up as to receive whatever he has for me. He places something on my tongue. It has weight, but no taste. I began to suck on it, move it about and eventually swallow it. But it's instantly replaced by more. I move it about and swallow it. Again, more simply appears in my mouth. More keeps coming. I can begin to see a bit of Jesus' face. I think he's smiling at me a bit amused. Some more comes into my mouth.

"Lord, what is this?"

"It is what you need. You might not recognize it, but it is what you need." Here comes some more.

"How much are you going to give me?"

"As much as you need." He smiles again almost enthusiastically. Here comes some more.

I now see what looks like a spoon, Jesus is using. He's spooning out of a cup and stirring it. "Lord, what's in the cup?"

"Something I've made especially for you. It's liquid love. Only I know how to make this. Take it." He lifts it up towards my face. He places it up to my mouth. I open my mouth and receive it. I wondered if this might produce some extraordinary experience. However, I can't say I feel anything much different, but do subtly witness something is at work within me. I sense the drink contains the power of his blood. Purification. He says, "Come drink."

"Lord I want to keep drinking more of you."

Jesus is fading back down to where he was before. I hear the crowd around me again. Over 5000 here, but he singled me out to give me something special.

At the end, I heard Him say regarding this experience, "And there's so much more, you're just at the beginning..."

Jesus Loves Us in Simple Ways Too

As I've been starting these exercises and seeking the Lord, I'm also starting to have "mini-visions". These are completely spontaneous and sometimes last for only seconds. Others are a bit longer.

One especially caught me by surprise. I suddenly saw Jesus in front of me, holding his hands up, cradling my face. He then began to stroke my head and my hair. I was dumbfounded and said, "Oh no Lord, I want to do this to you!" (I was thinking about something a friend shared with me how he went into a vision and was combing Jesus' hair...ministering to Him. I've wanted to do something like that so badly...) Jesus responded saying, "No, let me do this for you right now." He continued gently stroking down my head. Mind blowing. He was simply loving Me.

Revisiting Galilee — Jesus Provides Some Very Special Bread

I keep seeing glimpses of Jesus down by the lake of Galilee... I think I'm to go back there. "Lord is there anything else you wish to show me?"

I'm again aware of the grassy area, the people all around. I can see Jesus passing out bread. Oddly, unlike what I would expect from the biblical story, these are complete loaves. They're good sized, maybe 18 inches across and kind of flat, round. I even see marks in the top, like someone pressed something into the top for effect before baking. They're a nice, dark, golden brown. Jesus is handing them out.

"Do you want some?" the Lord asks.

"Well, of course Lord, I would like some".

I now see Him in front of me. He holds out a loaf. I take it, and break it in half. It's not as big as I thought; maybe about a foot across. It has a nice smell.

"Take and eat it".

I've been on a fast and haven't eaten any bread, but I will eat this. As I raise it up I can smell it. It's very fresh. I hold it up to my face and take a deep breath enjoying the aroma.

"Go ahead and eat it."

"OK Lord", but it was so enjoyable just looking at it, feeling it and smelling it. For some reason I hesitate, but start to eat it. It's almost like I realize, if I eat it, it will be gone. The smell will be gone, the lovely texture, the color... everything.

But I start to eat it. The crust is crunchy. The inside is moist and soft. I keep eating, but the loaf doesn't seem to disappear. I'm starting to get full, but the loaf is still there. I keep eating.

I see Jesus smiling at me. "It will never run out," He says.

"What I give you cannot be exhausted. It lasts forever. Eat and enjoy, I am not stingy. I don't know the meaning of that word. It doesn't exist in My Father's house. There is only abundance, more and more. You will never run out of Me. I have so much more for you yet."

I keep eating... it's as if I'm getting full, but it keeps on going someplace. I just keep eating more.

"Oh Lord, You are my everlasting supply."

"Of course I am", he says with a smile. "Now eat some more."

I start putting in two fistfuls at a time. It keeps on coming. It's almost like, as I fill up, I keep getting bigger, able to hold even more. "Lord, when is this going to stop?"

"Only I know. It is for you to just keep on eating. What I provide you must continue to eat. There's so much more."

I'm not consciously eating bread anymore. I'm just taking Him in. Come Lord Jesus... more of You. That's all that matters.

"What I give you, you must never turn down."

Reflections afterwards:
I have the impression that some things may not taste very pleasant at the time, but I must take them anyway. It reminds me of medicine. It was formulated by someone who knows what they are doing. We might not enjoy the taste, but it's for our benefit. Is this not how it is with the experiences of life? God has formulated everything. (I'm not saying bad experiences actually originate from the Lord. But if the enemy throws something at us, the Lord may allow us to be buffeted by it for a while.) Some things in life might not all taste good, but when I trust the Lord and consume what He has prepared for me, it has to be for my good. Thank you, Lord. I place my trust in you. Allow me to graciously accept all you have prepared for me. I repent and am sorry for those things I've resisted or rejected. I trust you and thank You. Amen.

Additional reflections about four months later:
My initial thoughts (as recorded above) centered on the necessity to pursue the Lord even during difficult times in our lives. We have to trust that He will ultimately create something good out of what we may perceive as a "difficult experience" in the present. Essentially this involves both trust and a choice on our part. If we choose to remain optimistic, knowing that God really is in control, it can ultimately lead to victory and peace in our lives. Paul obviously understood this when he testified, *"That is why, for Christ's sake, I delight in weaknesses, in insults, in hardships, in persecutions, in difficulties. For when I am weak, then I am strong."* (2 Corinthians 12:10)

Paul could *choose* to "delight" or rejoice in his sufferings because he had *absolute confidence* in God's goodness. Paul knew that no matter crossed his path, it didn't take God by surprise...and He could make something good out of the situation. However, if we choose to mope about in the desert as the Israelites frequently did, what good can come of that? We are effectively defeated already. When we really, really *understand in our hearts* that God is in control, we can only have confidence as a result.

All the above is Biblically harmonious truth. But I now realize that when the Lord made these statements, "What I provide you must continue to eat," and "What I give you, you must never turn down," also pertained to something else and very immediate.

In my pursuit of knowing the Lord intimately, I was always impressed with the experience of Moses. He spoke with God face to face, as one man speaks to a friend. The fact is we are living under a new, vastly superior covenant than what the Israelites lived under. Therefore, if Moses could have such clear, direct communication with the Lord, we should certainly have that kind of access as well. Yet, it's probably safe to say the vast majority of Christians have not experienced that level of direct intimacy. Why not?

Nonetheless, there seems to be an increasing number of testimonies of people being "caught up" as Paul was, not knowing if they were in or out of the body...and experiencing the things of heaven in a powerful way.

With my desire to experience the Lord in a most powerful way, I was also desirous of a similar experience. I wanted to experience Him face to face in a powerful, life changing way (and still do).

However, for the moment at least, the Lord has chosen a slightly different route to intimacy. Instead of having some kind of huge experience, He's illumined the teachings of Mark Virkler, Gary Oates and others bringing these to my heart's attention. And since the Lord has deemed it proper for me to start this way, it must be the best way for me to proceed.

Also, when examining my motives, I realized I wanted it all...and I wanted it now. In one sense there's nothing wrong with that desire, and I'm sure it pleases the Lord. However, He has chosen a different path, and I'm beginning to see why. Sometimes having a huge experience is the easy way. But in my life, it seems like the Lord has chosen the path of persistence.

If someone is taken into some kind of huge experience, it must be because that's what was best for them at the time. The Lord only does what's best for each of us. In my case, He has obviously wanted me to start with simple visions.

Despite the fact these started out "simple" doesn't mean they haven't been powerful. Some have not only been amazing to me, but when shared with others, have had significant impact as well.

Therefore, the statement, "What I give you, you must never turn down," has taken on additional meaning. What I am experiencing at the moment, might not be exactly what I was originally seeking, but it's a path the Lord has set before me, therefore I must wholeheartedly pursue it. And indeed, it has thus far been rewarding...

An Invitation

I was over at a small meeting of church friends tonight and shared the previous Galilee experiences. We spent some quiet time with the Lord before departing. In my mind, I was seeing things of nature. Then I had a more intense viewing of the seashore. This was not the Sea of Galilee, but was salt water... at least that was my distinct impression. I was down close to the wave line. I saw someone walking by in the sand...

Flashes of this persisted as I drove home. Does the Lord wish to meet with me there?

Now back at home: "Lord is there something you wish to show me?"

I hear the waves. My viewpoint is only inches above the waves as they slide in. They are gentle, only a few inches high, but they slide in and out perhaps 10 feet or so. I hear the waves, see a bit of foam. I see what appears to be sunlight glistening off the water. I'm aware of footsteps. I turn around and see a man in a long white robe walking along the edge of the sea. Is it Jesus? He smiles at me. He motions for me to follow him, using big, wide, overhead swoops with his arm.

I don't seem to go anywhere from here. It seems to stop for the moment. I sense it was an invitation to return. And return I shall...

[The continuation is entitled, "Jesus In Me" and occurred after the next experience...]

Allowing Jesus to Form Us

I was worshiping the Lord and saw hands forming bread. "Do you wish to say something to me Lord about this?"

I can see hands making bread. Small round, maybe six inches across, a couple inches thick. The hands are forming the loaves. I see the hands forming a loaf. There's flour on the surface of the work area. The hands appear to be just a bit on the older side, in other words, mature. There's a sense of experience here. The hands continue to form the loaf, sometimes slapping it about back and forth a bit. This is strange... the dough is now being shaped by slapping and it becomes thinner and thinner, almost like a pizza crust. ... maybe not quite that thin, but very close. Now it's bunched up again and then flattened into a finished loaf.

"Do you know what's happening here?" I am asked.

I reply, "Not really... someone's making bread."

"Yes, but something is being formed. Before the bread is baked it must be properly formed. If it is done incorrectly, it may collapse and fail. I know precisely how to form this loaf. And when I do it, it never fails. So it is with you. I know how to form you... it may not always seem pleasant that the time... You may feel like you're being slapped back and forth for no apparent reason. But there is a reason... and it's all part of my plan for the perfect loaf...you. You will be perfect and tasty, that is your destiny, but you must allow me to form you. If you become sticky or resistant, I must do even more work to get you perfectly formed. But if you just flow within my hands, the process will be so much smoother. Many will feast on your tastiness, but first you must be prepared.

And then there's the fire. The bread, like yourself, is never done unless it goes through the fire. I know the perfect temperature. I am not like a baker of this world that might burn, or undercook a loaf. My process is perfect."

"I thank you Lord, for your perfect attendance over my life. I'm sorry if I've been resistant to the molding you've attempted to do in my life. Right now Lord, I just want to yield to you. Thank You, Jesus."

Reflections afterward:
As I've come back to look at this again, I'm always struck by the last phrase, "My process is perfect." I know at the time, that phraseology took me by surprise. It didn't seem right in the context of the illustration. I would have expected Him to say something along the lines of, "I'm the perfect baker." But no, those words, "My process is perfect," is how He ended it. The emphasis seemed to be around the word "process" but not in the sense of a simple, step-by-step recipe. Rather, it was multidimensional; lots and lots of life experiences occurring and all coming together in an amazing way only He could engineer.

Jesus in Me!

I hear the waves. I'm back at the sea. This time I'm in the sand at the water's edge. I can feel the gentle waves. The water is pleasant, not cold. It feels nice. I see imprints of my hands in the sand as I pull them in and out. As I pull them away, the water swirls over the imprints. As the waves pull back, the imprints are partially filled in. I place my hands into the sand again and feel the water running over them. I sense Jesus a few feet away. He's wearing a long white robe. The water washes around his feet. He beckons to me with His hand. I take His hand and He lifts me up. He takes my hands. I can feel the strength in His hands. He's just looking at me and smiling. He runs his thumbs over the back of my hands. This just continues.

After a bit, I finally say, "Lord, do you want to tell me something?"

He smiles and just keeps looking at me. His presence is pleasant and peaceful, like having your best friend with you... even better than that.

"I do love you, you know..." He pauses. "Just come and spend more time with me."

His thumbs continue to message across the backs of my hands. He's smiling at me. I think He's simply enjoying this moment. I kind of wonder what's going on.

"Don't think every time we get together we have to have some "massive" experience... at least as the world thinks. I want more than anything to simply spend time with you. Just like this..." He continues to message the backs of my hands with his thumbs.

"Now I must tell you something. You are so precious to me. I see you like a gem on this seashore. You're beautiful, bright and polished. Don't fear what others think. They don't see you as I do. What I think is what really matters. Others must make their own decisions, but you have chosen the best thing, to simply stand here with me. I know what others think affects you, that's natural. But keep your eyes focused on me. I will never reject you, only love you."

Jesus seems to be getting brighter. He transfigures into a mass of light. "I am always with you. I will permeate your very being. Continue to draw close to me. I will fill you like you've never imagined or experienced. That's all that matters—you and I together. And together we will walk the path I have chosen for you."

I'm on my knees again in the sand at the water's edge. I stare at the imprints my hands make as the water washes in and out. I raise my hands and look at the moisture on my hands. It glistens in the light. It begins to glow and I see thin beams of light spreading out from the moisture glistening on my hand.

"That is Me within you... shining forth. I will wet those around you with My Spirit. They will be illumined. We will do this together."

I continue to look at my hands with these beams of light coming out. They now shine forth even more. The beams are bigger in diameter and a bit brighter. Some of the beams strike me in the face and they are pleasantly warm.

"You will radiate my Love to others."

"But Lord how I can do this? I'm so inadequate, still so bound up in my own problems." But as I'm saying this I'm instantly reminded of Moses' first conversation with God—and all the "problems" Moses thought he saw.

Yes, I know God will provide and mark the way. I just need to follow it.

I'm still looking at my hands with the beams coming out. Amazing. Jesus in me. Jesus in me...

Reflections afterwards:

Regarding Jesus' statement, "I know what others think affects you, that's natural." I found that remark interesting, because I'm not really influenced by what others think of me as much as it affects many other people. For example, I was generally not affected by peer pressure when I was young in school. I pretty much had a mind of my own. Nonetheless, nobody is completely immune to this sort of thing. As I meditate on this, I realize I do care what my closest friends think of me; I wouldn't want them to misunderstand me or my true intentions. However, I think this is encouragement from the Lord, that even if my closest friends push me away, or misunderstand my intentions, He will never do that. First and foremost, what He thinks is really the most important.

A Lesson in The Ways of the Spirit...

I got glimpses of Jesus again motioning for me to follow Him by the seashore.

I return to the seashore.

I continue to hear the waves. They seem a bit louder and just a bit larger than before. Again, I'm putting my hands into the sand. As I remove them, the waves wash over the handprints left behind.

"What do you see?" Jesus asks.

"I see the water washing back and forth, over my handprints in the sand. As the water retreats, little remains to be seen... just a soft depression. Another wave and the depression disappears completely."

Jesus is beside me, smiling. "What do you see?" He asks again.

I repeat, "I see waves washing over my hand prints... and they eventually disappear."

He smiles at me and says, "Look closer."

I see individual grains of sand being washed about. They seem to go this way and that way. You can't keep track of them though, as the waves come and go obscuring their view. I continue to hear the waves... It sounds so peaceful.

"Look again at the sand," Jesus says.

I notice that as the water washes over it, not all the water washes away. Some of it sinks into the sand. Jesus is still smiling.

"What does this all mean, Lord? What are you trying to tell me?"

"The sand is like your life. The grains are like individual events in your life. Things seem to go this way and that way. There doesn't seem to be any organization, no pattern. You can't see it, but it's there."

"What's there, Lord?"

"A completely organized plan for your life. You only see what is at the top. But as my Spirit sinks into your life, He permeates every incident in your life. The Spirit moves and organizes everything, though you might not recognize it."

I continue to watch the waves coming in and out.

"Is there anything else you wish to say to me about this Lord?"

He smiles at me again. "There is more; we'll discuss it later."

I still see and hear the waves, but sense this is over for the moment.

Reflections the next day:
As I woke the next morning, my thoughts turned again to this scene. I knew there was also meaning to the handprints in the sand, but was waiting to find out what it meant. As I meditated on this while lying in bed, I waited to see what might come.

I began to realize my handprints were my own efforts in trying to arrange the events in my life. I could push down hard, but to no avail. The water would come along and wash away my own self-effort. Even if I grasped and grabbed deeply into the sand, those efforts were washed away. A really deep hole might take a couple washings, but the result was always the same. The water... or the Spirit... always prevailed. I also note the process was always very gentle. The waves were always soft and gently washing, never violent and destructive like "human correction" can be.

I can think back to significant decisions and events in my life that I attempted to orchestrate myself. With some of these, I genuinely had the Lord in mind, but in hindsight these were revealed to be part of my own agenda. Deep though the holes were in the sand, those efforts were ultimately washed away. The sand was ultimately carried to where the Spirit wanted it to be. *"Many are the plans in a man's heart, but it is the Lord's purpose that prevails."*

(Proverbs 19:21)

The moral of the story? We need to relax, rest in Him and let the Spirit carry us along. Our own striving and effort will produce no lasting results in the Kingdom.

A further note: This kind of communication is new for me. I am not an abstract, allegorical kind of person at all. I prefer to think in clear, unmistakable, concrete terms. However, as Mark Virkler points out in his book, Jesus always communicated via pictures, in other words, parables. Yes, there were times he would come out and say something clearly and unambiguously, but that was not His first choice when teaching. Perhaps the pictorial approach draws us into meditation and spending more time with Him. I suspect this results in understanding at a deeper level that perhaps a simple, pat answer wouldn't achieve.

The Way of Man Versus the Way of God

In Mark Virkler's book, I just finished chapter 7, "Divine Patterns for Approaching God." In one place, he talks about the various pieces of furniture in the Tabernacle. I really sensed the presence and quickening of the Spirit while reading. The golden lampstand seems to have attracted my attention. I keep seeing Jesus standing next to it...

I see Jesus next to the lampstand. (The stand is to my left; Jesus is to the right.) The seven lamps are burning. One by one, from left to right, Jesus snuffs out the flames with His fingers. I hear a bit of a hiss as each is snuffed out. He stands back, raises His right hand and they all relight. His hand remains raised. And He's smiling at me. (I think He's enjoying all this along with my puzzlement. Such puzzlement must have been a common occurrence with the disciples too...)

"OK, Lord, what on earth are you trying to show me here? You know this abstract pictorial stuff is not easy for me."

"You must learn, and I will teach you. There is a whole new dimension of learning you have not yet experienced, but you will."

I still see Jesus standing by the lit lampstand with His hand raised.

"Is there something you want to tell me about this Lord?"

Jesus lowered his hand and folds his hands together. The flames seem to be brighter. I stand looking at this scene.

Jesus picks up the lampstand with His right hand and places it in front of me, between Himself and myself. He then holds both sides of the stand, his hands wrapped palms up, around the outer branches.
He now releases it. I see bright light emanating from where Jesus was behind the stand. The stand is silhouetted in front of the bright light. I now see His hands again stretching out from the light.

(Jesus says) "I and the way, the truth and the life."

I feel myself being drawn closer towards the lampstand and Jesus. The light becomes brighter. It's almost as if the lampstand — with the light of Jesus behind it — come into and overwhelm me

I'm in the light. It's warm, almost hot. Light is everywhere. I'm just immersed in the light.

Reflections afterwards:
I just remained in His presence for a while experiencing His Unmistakable Peace. At the same time, I'm puzzled by what I saw. In my earlier visions, explanations seemed to come quickly. In my last vision of the seashore, however, fuller revelation didn't come until the next morning when I awoke and meditated on what I saw. Now I'm left... at the moment... without really understanding much of anything.

I also sense it's a test... simply write down what comes, even if I can't make immediate sense of it (it's not easy — my brain wants to get in the way) and trust Him for the revelation in due time.

As I awoke the next morning I lay in bed pondering this, looking again at what happened. I've been thinking about what I saw and making observations...

Snuffing out the candles one by one: It occurs to me that's how man would have lit the lamps. A person would stand in front, start on one side and light the lamps one at a time. Jesus snuffed them out in the same manner they were lit... but then relit them His way... supernaturally. He didn't even have to touch them, or light a match. All He did was raise His hand and by His will and power, they all relit together; clearly a supernatural act.

After He relit the lamps, He put the lamp stand to use. This may also speak to man's efforts. The lamp stand was of God's design — but man attempted to light it his way. Instead God desired to light it all at once by His power. Only then was the lamp stand put to use.

It seems in the church today, we spend a lot of energy creating and engaging in all sorts of programs—most often of our own design. However, in the Old Testament, the tabernacle was not designed by man, but by God. He gave instructions to Moses, who then supervised its construction, guaranteeing everything was made according to the plan God designed. After God's design was implemented and the Ark of the Covenant set in place, the manifested power and presence of God appeared in the midst of the people. A new era in God's relationship with man had begun.

In contrast, how often in our churches today do we diligently seek to hear God's voice *and carry out the plans He desires?* Or do we simply instigate plans of our own design...and hope they accomplish something?

For example, generally accepted wisdom regarding church planting says a church building needs to be highly visible on a main street...and if possible at intersecting roads. The usual reasoning is, the more visible the church, the more likely people might stop by.

However, John Wimber, who pastored the first Vineyard Fellowship, violated every rule in the book when it came to church planting. Instead, he sought out God's plan. The Lord led him to rent a large, unused warehouse in the middle of an industrial park. Such a location offered little public exposure, yet within a few years, the church became a megachurch with thousands in attendance. How was that possible?

It was possible, because God was obviously in it. Many sought out the Vineyard because people experienced the manifest presence of God there. Many were miraculously healed and saved. Just as in Jesus' ministry, when the power of God is manifested, people come, regardless of the location.

To see the manifest power of God, we need to seek out His will, His plan and carry it out as He wishes—not how we *think* it should be done.

But even if we make mistakes and stray off the path, He's always there ready and willing to guide us back, if we listen and submit to His will. And if we are honestly seeking Him, His correction is not brutal like some earthly taskmaster.

I noticed when Jesus snuffed out the lamps, he did so gently. His attitude was not like "Oh, this is all wrong..." and then curtly put out the lamps. Rather, it was done in a gentle, but deliberate manner.

The Woodland Garden

I see a large fountain of water bubbling up. It seems to be coming out of pool surrounded by rocks, plants and trees... almost like a natural garden. The upwelling of water is maybe 4-6 inches across and bubbles up from the surface maybe six inches. It's quite cold. I stick my head over it and take in a little of the water. I can feel the cool on my face and the cold on my teeth. The water is very pure. I hear a little burbling noise as it rises up and bubbles forth.

"Do you know what you are drinking?" a voice asks.

I see a figure in a glowing white robe, seemingly standing on the surface of the water just behind the bubbling water.

"Do you know what you are drinking?" he again asked.

"It's very nice, crystal clear, cold water," I reply.

I look up at the glowing figure again; it's Jesus smiling at me.

"Taste it again."

I bend over and taste the cool water... it's very refreshing.

"You get so hot and bothered with things," the Lord says. "I have this spring here for you always. It's always available for you to drink from. The cares of the world, the fears, the uncertainties; this water can sooth and wash them all away. I provide this as a gift for you. Come often and drink from it. I've made it just for you."

I drink some more. As I do, I sense the thought "liquid peace".

I am aware of some small trees to my left; they look like miniature birches, but the leaves are almost a glowing green.

"I wish I could see more of this Lord."

"All you have to do is ask", he smiles.

I sense and hear more noises from the garden and woods. But the noises are not like those heard in ordinary woods. These have a palpable life to them... almost like a substance, it's hard to explain.

"What is this place, Lord?"

"It is a part of what I have prepared for you...but you are seeing only a very little piece of it."

I wish I could see more clearly. I get glimpses of beams of light shining through the leaves of trees and plants. I smell a freshness in the air, it too is full of life.
I'm aware of grass I'm kneeling on. It's beautiful green, soft, uncut, about four or five inches high.

I'm suddenly aware of a bench over to my right, by the right side of the pool. It appears to be made of light stone. It has little sparkles to it. I get up and sit on the bench... Jesus is still standing on the water in middle of the pool. I can't quite make out how big the pool is... it seems to meander off into the woods.

Lord, I'd like to come back here and explore a bit more, if that's OK."

He smiles, says nothing but I sense he's pleased. I look again at the bubbling waters. I quick get up, have another drink then return and sit on the bench.

Suddenly I see something large and orange to my right, about ten or fifteen feet away. It appears to be a large flower of some kind. It's not yet open, but a huge bud. There's green foliage below, a stem about eighteen inches high and a huge orange bud, swollen perhaps a foot across and maybe two feet high.

What's this Lord?

"It's a surprise." He answers. "Keep watching it."

It seems to swell bigger. It suddenly bursts open. It has large petals on the outside like a magnolia, but the inside is dense, more like a rose or camellia, but it's huge. It's giving off multiple fragrances... I know this, but it's like I can only smell a bit of it. It's as if I don't have the ability to smell it in all its fullness. What I can detect is fresh and sweet. It's hard to explain, but it's almost like life itself is emanating from it. I saw what seemed like some kind of insect fly around and into it... and suddenly the flower snapped shut! ...and now it seems to remain that way.

I wonder at all this. I'm sitting on the bench looking out over the water as Jesus is still there, smiling.

"It is a treasure," Jesus says. "Think about it."

"Ok Lord."

I know the place is beautiful, but as in many of my visions, I can't always see clearly in intense detail, rather almost foggy. It's ended for now. I am reminded of what the apostle Paul said about we only see now as in a glass, darkly. I've been asking the Lord to see much more clearly and had the sense, that in time, I shall.

God Provides What We Need at This Moment

I've continued to get glimpses of the bubbling water throughout the day. I sat down for a bit in the afternoon and was able to revisit the garden. I was talking to the Lord about the fact it's hard to see clearly. The stuff with the flower... was that really Him, or my imagination? I really would like to see some concrete fruit from these visions... otherwise one has to question their validity. I've been frank with the Lord about this. I don't want to be wasting my time, or misled.

In any case, I was looking over the scene again. I suddenly realized what I was really looking at. Originally, I thought it was a small pond that sort of meandered away into the distance. I now realize it's the head of a spring. The "pond" is just a small area around the spring's origin, (perhaps about 15 feet across) and then the water is actually flowing away from there. I don't know why I didn't realize this sooner. [Especially when Jesus identified it as a spring in the previous vision!]

I bent down over the water again and was washing my face with the upwelling water. To my surprise, it was warm! I could feel some gentle heat rising from the surface. It seemed to be the same, pure water, but this time it was warm.

I got a glimpse of the bench again over to the right. However, the large orange flower bud was now between me and bench — it had moved. Before, it was beyond the bench, to my right some distance when I had been seated.

Who ever heard of a flower moving by itself from one place to another? Who ever heard of a spring that's cold at one time, then warm at another? This is obviously no ordinary garden. I sense that though this place has a design to it, it's not static, like an earthly garden. I also get the sense it adapts to my needs of the moment. Very interesting. It's like when I drank from the spring, it was cold. But when I wanted to splash the water in my face, it was warm! I have the impression this speaks to the provision of the Lord. He's always got what we need at the moment. I'll definitely have to revisit this and see what else the Lord might be showing me...

The Passage of Time:
Our Perspective Versus God's

I've been having glimpses of the sea shore again and seeing a boat... I've been so busy and my computer's been tied up many days with maintenance tasks, so I haven't been journaling like before. But I know I need to. This morning my computer was available and I decided not to put it off...

I'm back at the seashore. The waves are gently moving in and out. I sense Jesus standing close by. I'm also aware of a boat, seemingly moored about 20 feet offshore. The sun glistens off the water behind the boat.

Jesus says, "Come I want to show you something."

I've been stooping down close to the water, but now stand up. Jesus is out in front of me, his form somewhat silhouetted by the sun. He's by my left side and takes my left hand. We start to walk out into the water towards the boat. It's crudely made, hand hewn and very shallow in comparison to boats I'm familiar with. I climb inside. Jesus is out in front, still out in the water and starts to pull the boat forward. He faces forward, towing the boat with his right hand behind him. I hear the water sloshing around Jesus' feet. The boat is well worn. A little water rolls about in the bottom. My bottom side gets a bit wet from the water. Jesus is pulling me into deeper water. It's up to his waist, now his chest. As he's pulling me along, suddenly we've arrived somewhere. He's come up out of the water, his clothes all wet. I'm now standing outside the boat on shore. The sun still glistens in the background.

Jesus says, "I've just taken you a journey. Do you know where you are?"

"No Lord."

"You're about a thousand miles away from where we started."

That didn't seem possible. It seemed only as if Jesus had walked a short distance. It took only seconds not even minutes. I see a few small pillars of rock by the shore. Although we are in a sandy spot, there are many more rocks in this place than where we had been—it's definitely different.

"So it is with your life." Jesus says. "What looks like a lengthy, formidable journey to you, can take just seconds with me. You look at the pace at which things have been going. But my pace is different. In a moment of time I can accomplish what might take you a lifetime of striving in your own strength."

"But Lord, I've been trying to give things to you. Some things just don't seem to be progressing at all."

"I know," Jesus answers. "But that's from your perspective. I need you to trust me... and my perspective."

"OK Lord," I begin to cry. "But it's so hard."

"Don't worry." He says. "Remember what I've told you before. I will never hurt you or leave you. As you placed your trust in me, while I pulled the boat, I need you to trust me now."

I hug Him and He hugs me. I weep.

"It's so hard, Lord, but I will try to trust you."

"Ah," Jesus says, "you already are! Don't you think I see that? And I love you for it. Yes, it's hard, but you *are* trusting me. There are those who do not. I continue to woo them, but they do not respond as you have."

"Lord, I'm so aware, of my lack of trust. I guess there's always room for improvement."

"Of course," he says, "but you're doing just fine. Keep on persevering. I gave you that teaching on perseverance for a reason. You will be sharing it with others. But your teaching will be so much more powerful when backed up by what I have done for you."

"I bless you, Doug."

I see Jesus standing there, still all wet. Yet even after we hugged, I'm still dry... well, except for my wet bottom from the boat. Go figure.

"Lord, who else is as trustworthy as you? I'll keep grabbing hold. Who is there besides you?"

I'm not sure if the vision is ending or not. I sense there's more...

"Is there anything else you want to show me at this time, Lord?"

I found myself back in the boat again. But suddenly, we were in the middle of a jungle...with me still in the boat and Jesus out in front. Then we seemed to suddenly move from place to place. I got glimpses of other places, including one where we were surrounded by a white, icy landscape. All the time, I'm still in the boat, with Jesus out front.

Jesus says, "No matter where we go, I will always be at the helm."

An Unexpected Encounter:
We Have Friends We Don't Know About

I'm back at the seashore. The gentle waves are washing in and out. The golden sun glistens across the water. I wait.

I look up into the sky. It fades out into a dark, inky blue. Overhead, I can see a few stars. It's almost an ethereal landscape. The sun is at the horizon, yet I can make out stars overhead in the dark, ink blue sky. I'm down at the water's edge. I'm on my knees, the waves washing in and out over my hands. I can hear the gentle sound of the water as it rolls in and out. A stronger current of water swishes by me from the right. I sense someone standing to my right. It's Jesus.

"What do you see?" he asks.

"A beautiful scene, the sun in the distance, glistening off the water."

"Now listen," Jesus says.

I continue to hear the waves washing in and out, as they wash around my hands. My knees and feet are also getting wet as I'm kneeling.
I keep listening.
I then hear someone calling out in the distance... somewhere out at sea. It sounds like they are calling for help.

Shall we go look?" Jesus asks.

Suddenly the boat from my previous experience is there. I climb in and Jesus is out in front pulling the boat. He pulls us out to sea, but oddly he never seems to sink much deeper than His waist.

I can hear the voice getting louder. It's definitely someone calling out for help.
I can see a figure out in the water, waving his hand in the air calling out. Jesus pulls the boat up towards him.

"I'm so glad you found me," the man exclaims. "I thought I was lost." I help the man into the boat with Jesus also extending a hand.

The man is now sitting in the boat with me, facing me, cross-legged in the bottom of the boat. He is all wet, including his hair, but smiling. He's wearing what appears to be a rough, natural color robe. It's very basic; almost like a working garment.

"Who are you?" I ask.

"A friend," he replies.

"A friend?" I wonder. "Do I know you?"

"Yes and no," he replies. That's a strange answer.

I don't recognize him, but he seems to be a very nice person. It's hard to describe, but he almost exudes a sense of friendliness, something palpable you can feel, as he sits there smiling.

"I met you a long time ago," he says. "Really?" I say. "And where was that?"

He looks at Jesus seemingly unsure what to say. It's as if he and Jesus know each other. "Shall we let him in?" the man asks. Jesus nods yes.

"Take my hands," he says, reaching out. I take them. They're cool and wet from the water. He sits there smiling at me.

I'm completely puzzled. "Who is this?" I wonder to myself. The man again looks at Jesus and then back at me. It's as if they know something between them.

"I'm someone who cares a great deal about you."

"Are you an angel?" I ask.

"No, not exactly," he replies. "I'm someone who's gone on before you."

I continue to hold his wet, cool hands. He keeps looking over at Jesus, smiling and looks back. "I've been assigned to you. I pray for you."

I don't seem to go any further at this point... the vision fades. This is very puzzling.

Reflections afterwards:
At the beginning, the appearance of the seascape would suggest this was not of this world. To have the sun at horizon and yet have such a dark sky overhead is not the way skies at sunset typically look here on earth. It had a surrealistic beauty to it.

Why introduce this man to me in such a strange way? I now sense he wasn't really lost, but was placed there to introduce me — but what a strange, almost bizarre way to introduce someone. The fact he was sopping wet was very palpable.

One thing that occurs to me: I had a sense many years ago, that my coming to the Lord was at least partially the result of someone praying for me; possibly an old relative, or friend I was too young to know as a child.

Might there be a connection here? It is generally acknowledged we all have angels assigned to minister to us. I've often thought that when we get to heaven we would still be praying for those we've left behind... Why not? It would seem a reasonable thing we would want to do. Apparently, those who have gone on before us cannot generally interact with us here on earth. However, there are accounts of people who have temporarily visited heaven and encountered relatives there, or others such as the apostle Paul, Moses, etc.

What I initially come away with is this: Yes, there are angels here to minister to us in the here and now, but there are others in heaven, praying for us as well.

I will admit while this was occurring I had concerns. The Bible has clear admonitions against communicating with the dead. However, I did not instigate this. Like heavenly encounters shared in the book, "Heaven is Real", the Lord instigated the encounter. The little boy in that book did not seek communication or information from the dead. However, he was introduced to two relatives that had gone on before him. The Lord apparently sanctioned that for the purpose of encouragement...and testifying to the reality of heaven.

Another observation; when writing this I had another glimpse of this man in the boat, with Jesus behind him. However, it was if I could see Jesus right through the man. At no time was there any attempt to take my attention off Jesus and put it exclusively on this man. Rather it's as if the life and love of Jesus was shining through him. In fact, that's scripturally sound. Our ultimate goal is to get out of the way and so others see Jesus in us. Having this overt focus on Jesus also helped put my mind at ease regarding this vision.

I also intend to meditate on the environment surrounding this vision. Might there be some additional meanings to the things I saw?

Further reflections a few weeks later:
Two significant things have occurred since having this vision. I finally unpacked the last box after moving to a new home earlier this year. Inside I came across a brand new (but as yet unpublished) book given to me last year by my friend Mike Rogers. In fact, it's more like a scholarly paper than a book. Entitled "When Heaven Touches Earth," the purpose is to give scriptural authentication to experiences like I've been having. Of particular interest; a significant section dealt with encounters involving "those who've gone before." It provides both scriptural and contemporary examples of such encounters. It also details a number of tests to ensure they are genuine. My vision easily passed these tests as illustrated by the following:

1. The encounter was instigated by the Lord, not myself. I was resolutely seeking Him and Him alone.
2. The experience has born good fruit in my spirit, such as joy and peace (Matt 7:15-27; Gal 5:22-23).
3. It provided edification and comfort (1Cor 14:3).

4. The vision ultimately pointed to and glorified Jesus (Rev 19:10).

In my previous comments I said, *"I also intend to meditate on the environment surrounding this vision. Might there be some additional meanings to the things I saw?"*

One evening while meditating on the vision, a memory suddenly popped into my head I hadn't thought of in years. It was quite prominent. I was with my mother, brother and some friends vacationing at a lake in northern Wisconsin. Late one afternoon, I went out in a rowboat perhaps 50 feet offshore to do some fishing. I was only about 9 or 10 years old.

As dinnertime was approaching, I pulled up the anchor to go ashore. However, the anchor had become encased in heavy mud. I could raise it up to the rim of the boat, but couldn't get it inside. It was much too heavy. There was no way for me to hold the rope with one hand and pull the anchor up and over into the boat with the other — it was simply too heavy. I therefore let it drop, hoping to wash off the mud. I tried over and over, but simply could not get it up and over inside the boat... and now I was getting tired, embarrassed and very frustrated with myself...and feeling terrible.

My mother finally came out on the pier to call me in for the meal. Initially, she didn't know what to do about my predicament. We had only the one boat. However, there was a single man next door who somehow became aware of the problem. He got into his boat, rowed out and came alongside me.

I remember him smiling. I think he sensed my embarrassment and frustration. I don't remember much, except he was very nice and gently dismissed the circumstance, saying something like "these things just happen sometimes." He was able to grab the anchor and set it inside the boat. I hope I thanked him... I really don't remember. However, I was quick to get back to shore, still quite embarrassed and frustrated with myself.

I also recall, a few days later he brought over some freshly caught fish for us to eat. I remember my mother referring to him as "the man who rescued you".

Could this be the man I met in the vision? Could the struggling young boy have touched his heart? There are some interesting things to note:

- This memory seemingly just popped up out of nowhere while contemplating the vision.
- When in the vision I asked the man, "Do I know you?" his answer would certainly fit this circumstance: "Yes and no. I met you a long time ago."
- Then there are interesting parallels. In my childhood, a man came out in a boat and rescued me. In the vision, with Jesus leading the way, I went out in a boat and "rescued" a man. My childhood rescuer would have gotten his hands wet when pulling up the anchor. I specifically felt the wet hands of the man in the vision.

Is all of this coincidence? I might never have a definitive answer this side of eternity. However, it can still illustrate the incredible ways the Lord can weave together events in our lives in ways we could *never possibly* imagine...

Whoever Believes in Me Will Do the Works I Have Been Doing

(John 14:12)

I read the account of blind Bartimaeus in Mark earlier in the day. While taking a shower this evening I started seeing what appeared to be a vision of something similar. I saw lots of people on a dusty road. I also seemed to see the Lord stepping out of crowd, walk towards me, lay his hands on me and then scales fell from my eyes.

Later, I was sitting down and praying...
"Lord Jesus, do you want to show me something here?"

I'm on a dry, dusty road. I'm aware of a lot of people around me, many talking to each other. It's a bright sunny day with a blue sky. I continue to hear the noise of the crowd around me. I hear a commotion behind me and turn around. Someone is traveling down the road and people are taking note. Someone to my right is standing up, peering over others' heads trying to see who it is. People start to walk away from where I am, following this person. I elect to walk along. I suspect it is Jesus. I can see him walking purposefully forward, with others following behind. He continues walking at a good pace.

This just seems to continue on and on and I'm wondering what's happening. What's the purpose here? In my spirit, it's as if I hear the Lord encouraging me to keep on watching.

He continues to walk purposely forward at a good pace. I now see hands raised by some following behind, as if they are trying to get the man's attention — but he keeps walking resolutely forward.

This continues and I keep on watching. I'm kind of walking sideways and off to the side watching all this. But then I stumble on a small rock and fall. Suddenly the man stops, looks in my direction and come over to me. I'm certain it must be Jesus. He offers me a hand and helps me to my feet. He reaches down with his hands and helps dust me off.

"Is that better?" He asks.

"Yes, Lord. But what's going on here?"

"Just follow me," he says. So, I fall in just behind his right side and continue to walk. He continues to walk along at a good, deliberate speed.

Suddenly he stops. On the road in front of him sits a man. Jesus asks, "Friend, what can I do for you?"

The man motions with his hands, but cannot speak clearly. Just "ahhs" and "uuhs" come from his mouth. Jesus stoops down on one knee in front of him. He looks at the man and places his hand on the man's head. The man starts to call out, almost as if in pain…louder. He calls out again. "Aiyeeeee!" "Ahh!" He breathes heavily and then starts to relax as Jesus holds his head, now with both hands. The man looks at Jesus, winces a bit and lets out a hack. He now looks in amazement and then begins to weep. Jesus folds him in his arms and comforts him. Jesus then helps him to his feet. The crowd murmurs with apparent wonderment.

The man starts to laugh, with Jesus still holding on to him.

Jesus looks over to me and says, "Come here." So, I come closer and He says, "This man was a prisoner, but now he's been set free. You will be doing the same thing in my name." I stand in wonderment, together with Jesus and the man—his eyes fixed on Jesus, radiantly joyous.

"Lord, what did you do for this man?" I ask.

"He was held prisoner by the enemy for 32 years," he responds, "but has now been set free."

The man is now jumping about in exuberant joy, laughing and clapping his hands together over his head in the air.

"You will do the same things because I am in you," Jesus says. "Sometimes you may not feel like it, but it is true. Remain in me, as I choose to remain in you."

I am reminded of the vine; it can bear no fruit apart from the root. And Jesus must remain my root.

I then ask, "Lord, earlier in the shower, I thought I saw you stepping up to me, placing your hands on me and scales falling from eyes. Was that really from you?"
"Yes, it was," he replies. "I am about to reveal even more of my kingdom to you. But you must remain close to me. The enemy would like to destroy you, but he cannot. I will protect you. I have paid a heavy price for you and will never let anything harm you. Again, remain in me as I have chosen to remain in you."

Reflections afterwards:
The fact Jesus was walking so swiftly forward suggested a purposeful destination. He wasn't just casually walking along with his disciples. It was almost as if he had an appointment and wanted to reach it.

The fact the man was sitting in the road, not alongside it, is interesting. Might he have deliberately placed himself there, right in the middle of path, knowing Jesus was coming that way? Was Jesus aware of this and that's why he was deliberately pressing forward?

It was interesting that when I stumbled and fell, Jesus immediately took notice, came over and helped me. This despite the fact there were many others around vying for his attention and that he was pressing forward in a determined fashion. I have a sense he wanted me to see what was going to happen; that's why I was brought there and He didn't want me left behind.

It was interesting watching this. In the Gospels, explanations are always provided for the reader during the narrative. In this case however, I had no explanations... I was just watching it unfold before me.

The fact the crowd murmured when the man was helped to his feet was interesting. I knew nothing about this man, but apparently others in the crowd did know him. The fact he was standing up straight was apparently significant. I didn't get the impression he was physically incapacitated, but perhaps an impure spirit was interfering with his mobility in addition to his speech.

I was hoping Jesus would fill me in with more details, but he only added the fact this had lasted 32 years. He seemed content I be aware the man had been a prisoner of the enemy and was now free... and that I would be doing the same things with Him in the future.

Twice Jesus said, "Remain in me as I have chosen to remain in you." As He said this, it was imparted to me just what He meant. He has already chosen to live in us; that's a "done deal." However, we must *continually choose* to remain in Him.

He will never, ever walk away from us. However, in a manner of speaking, it's possible for us to walk away from Him. He's given us the freedom to try doing things our way, if we choose. Of course, that invariably leads to problems and frustrations. However, by choosing to remain in Him, i.e., doing things His way, we are guaranteed ultimate success, fulfillment and victory. Amen!

The Choice Is Ours

I've been so busy this last week. So many distractions.

I've been getting images of the Lord standing out in the middle of a busy street. Cars zooming back and forth. I've seen it several times. I began to realize it tied in with my busyness in the last several days. I noticed that as the hustle bustle of cars sped back in forth in front of me, they would obscure Jesus. I could only see flashes of Him in between all the cars. I begin to realize this is what happens when we let the busyness of life get between us and Jesus. We can no longer see Him clearly...we only catch glimpses of Him from time to time.

I don't like this. I want to see Him clearly, not like this. "Lord, what must I do to stop all this?"

"Come to me. Come to me first. It takes training. You must learn, that no matter what is going on, it can all wait. I am always standing here waiting for you."

I put up my hands and focus on Jesus. The cars stop. I can now see Him standing before me.

"Lord, I'm sorry. I should have done this much sooner."

"I know," He says. "But now you have done it." He takes my hands and looks at me with understanding.

At one point, a few cars tried to start moving again, but I immediately stopped them. I choose... I will to see Jesus and Him alone. All that other stuff is secondary. Jesus must come first...

A Lesson in God's Provision

I'm standing in a running brook... maybe 20-30 feet across. There are many stones about. It's not a waterfall, but the water is running around and over the rocks. I stoop down and place my hands in the water and can feel it running over my hands. It's cool, but not cold. Jesus is standing a few feet away, out in front of me. The water is running around his feet and catches the bottom of his robe. As I'm stooping down feeling the water, Jesus takes my hands and lifts me up.

I stand facing Him. We seem to be in a wooded area, though it's not really dense woods. It's open where we are, but I can catch glimpses of a few fir trees around us. I can hear the water running over the rocks and around our feet.

"Lord, is there something you want to tell me here?"

I continue to hear the sound of the water running around us.

"Listen," Jesus says.

In addition to the water, I hear a lone bird whistling, not far away. His song is beautiful, cheery. Suddenly he lands on a rock in the stream. He takes in some water and flies off again. (His color was gray, similar in appearance to a mockingbird.) I can still hear him singing.

"Did he have to spend a lot of time looking for this water?" Jesus asks. "No, it's all around him. All he had to do was land in it, take a sip and off he went. He didn't have to spend a great deal of time searching for it. It's here in abundance for him."

I can still hear the bird singing somewhere not far away.

"So it is with my provision in your life. It's not far away. It's flowing all around you. You just need to stop, let it flow around you and take a sip. Take as much as you need, because it is inexhaustible."

I still hear the bird singing a little distance away, but am now also aware of a breeze springing up. My clothes are ruffled, and Jesus's robe moves about in the breeze.

Again, I see the bird. He's flying about and riding on the currents within the breeze.

"So, it is with your life," Jesus says. "My spirit is always here to refresh you, to buoy you up as you go from place to place."

I see the bird flying about; he's not fighting against the puffs of breeze, but rather moving with them, sliding among the currents in the breeze. He obviously had no cares. The breeze was around him... and whenever he wished he could have a sip of the nice cool, water below.

Jesus is holding my hands as we continue to watch the bird fly about.

I suddenly thought I saw what might be a bird of prey swooping down towards the little bird flying about. I think to myself, "Is this real? Surely the Lord is not going to show me this little bird being devoured." As I was wrestling with this, my neighbor's dog began barking interrupting the vision. I tried coming back to it... Again, I saw what might have been a bird of prey swooping down... and the neighbor's dog started barking again. It was all very disconcerting and distracting. I couldn't see much anymore. However, I waited.

After a few moments pass by, I can now see myself in the stream again with Jesus.

"Things will try to attack and distract you. That too is part of life in this world. However, throughout that distraction, I was still here holding your hands." I can feel His strong hands holding mine.

"I will never let you go," Jesus says.
"I will **never** let you go," He repeats with emphasis.

The dog starts to bark again and Jesus just smiles. "Just let him try to interrupt us...he cannot. I intend to bless you and nothing, no power can stop that."

The dog continues to bark. But Jesus places His hand on my head. "I bless you with all that is mine," He says with a smile. "Nobody can take this from you. It is my gift to you."

I feel His hand on my head. There is power in His hand. It's not just physical, but spiritual.

The neighbor's dog is silenced.

"Now receive." He says. "My peace I give to you. My strength I give to you."

He now has both hands holding my head. I can feel something coming in. It's hard to describe, but it's sort of like peace and power mixed together.

It's as if Jesus starts to get brighter...and then brighter and then disappears revealing the sun behind him... I now see the bright sun in the sky as I continue to see the beautiful scenery around me with the stream at my feet.

As the vision ends, I can still feel something tangible entering me...

Reflections afterwards:
This statement drew my additional attention:
"So it is with my provision in your life. It's not far away. It's flowing all around you. You just need to stop, let it flow around you and take a sip. Take as much as you need, because it is inexhaustible."

This year has been fiscally very tight for me. So when first hearing this, my natural inclination was to think in terms of financial provision. However, I sensed in my spirit, that was not the focus here, but rather the Lord was referring primarily to spiritual provision. After all, everything connected to our well-being originates in the spirit, not the flesh. Everything flows out from the spirit. A person can have little money, but still be at peace and fulfilled.

All this reinforces the necessity to remain focused on the Lord, not our apparent problems and shortfalls. Ultimately, He is the source of our peace and fulfillment, not the circumstances of life, despite the fact they can be in our face demanding attention. It all comes down to trust: Trusting that He has already provided for us and will see us through the difficult, noisy circumstances in life.

Another interesting note regarding the barking dog and ensuing interruption: When Jesus said, *"Just let him try to interrupt us... he cannot,"* I distinctly sensed He was not literally referring to just the dog. This was no coincidence. Rather, it was a direct manifestation of the enemy trying to interfere. But Jesus confidently proclaimed, *"he cannot..."* The enemy is utterly powerless in the presence of Jesus. And once Jesus determined there would be no more interruption, there was none!

"Follow Me"

I felt led to read through everything I've seen and written so far. I hadn't read about the garden for a while. However, I noticed I had asked Jesus if I could see more...and he responded all I had to do is ask. I remember asking at the time, but subsequent visions went elsewhere. However, this evening when reading that account, I asked again. I seem to be getting glimpses of something new...

I'm back in the garden. I'm trying to look around and see everything I previously saw, but my attention seems to be guided in a different direction. I never saw anything behind me before, but now I'm noticing a path at the edge of the pool that winds away from the pool. As I stand trying to look across the pool, I'm not seeing much very clearly. Instead the focus is on the path. It comes to the edge of pool where I stand and leads away. At present that's the clearest thing I can see.

The path seems to be a light brown, earthen path. On either side, I see tufts of beautiful, fresh, soft green grass. It's perhaps 6 inches high along the edges of the path. The path seems to wind its way through a clearing.

I've turned around away from the pond and am looking down at the path. I seem to have on dark shoes (though I can't see them clearly) and white trousers.

"Lord, what am I to do here?" I ask.

I hear wind blowing through the trees. It's as if there's a voice in the wind saying, "Follow me."

I can see wind swirling through the trees and there seems to be a bright light behind them, but it's not a point, like the sun, rather it seems to be in the air behind the trees. It's as if the light and wind are somehow related.
I can't really see all that clearly, but I can see the path well enough to start walking down it. I feel a warm breeze coming at me. I've walked just a short distance from the pond, through a clearing, but can see some trees ahead.

The trees are not particularly large; the trunks are no more than a foot or so in diameter. They might be 30 feet high. I can't see any leaves...it's hard to see detail as I'm looking into the light. It's much brighter now, coming from behind the trees.

I come closer to the edge of the trees. There's a gentle breeze coming towards me, slightly warm. The light is warm. I step up to the edge of the wood. I can't see any further because of the bright light.

"Follow Me," the voice says again.

I sense the light in front of me. It's almost palpable. I put my hands up and can feel what seems like a thin, flexible barrier. It's warm.

I elect to step through.

Suddenly I'm somewhere else. There's light everywhere. I sense someone standing over to my left, and a bit out in front. I'm not sure if it's an angel or the Lord. I can see only from the waist on down...he's wearing a white robe and what appears to be sandals. From the waist up, he vanishes into the light.

He extends a hand out towards me, which I take with my left hand.
Although there's lots of light around, it appears slightly dimmer straight ahead.

"Come with me," I hear again.

Suddenly the person stands straight out in front of me. His eyes are glowing with light. He smiles at me.

"I want to take you on a tour," he says. He draws me close and puts his arms around me. He is full of warmth and power. I now see an area of very bright light behind him. He hugs me and the light comes closer and surrounds us. I feel as if my own person is almost like a dark hole in comparison to all this light.

"Don t be afraid," he says.

"Ok Lord, do what you want to do with me."

It seems to be ending for the moment. The whole thing was both interesting and frustrating. As I was seeing this unfold, I was also aware I was simultaneously in my chair, eyes closed and typing everything as it happened. It's like being in two places at once and somewhat distracting. It's like the physical side is restricting what's happening, almost like an anchor holding a boat in place.

Well Lord, you know what's going on here. I've already given it all to you. As always, it's up to you to initiate the next step, whatever that might be.

A few notes some months later...
When entering a vision, I'm always sure to do something Gary Oates teaches: look around. By willfully looking around one might see something they might otherwise miss. In this vision, I tried to look around the pool in the garden. However, there are times the Spirit directs the focus and that's what we primarily see. Although there were other familiar things in this garden, I wasn't able to focus on them. Instead, the path was presented to me. It was the clearest thing I saw and therefore elected to follow it. Nonetheless, I still try to look around and record anything I see. In this case, I recorded the nature of the path and what I was wearing. I've occasionally discovered seemingly insignificant details can take on significance when later reviewing a vision. So I make a practice of "looking" and then recording what I see.

Little did I realize the practice of "looking around" would become the central activity in my next experience...

The Tour Begins

(a follow-up of the previous vision)

I see a bright radiating light out in front of me in my mind's eye. However, I need to keep my eyes open to see it. When I close my physical eyes, I can't see it. Odd.
Jesus is in the light. I can see his arms extending outward. At first, I cannot make out anything other than His arms. But now I'm beginning to make out some other features. His hair seems to have some brown to it. He's wearing a white robe, with very loosely fitting sleeves. He's smiling.

"I'm here to take you on your tour," He says. He puts His hands on my shoulders. I can feel the strength in His hands. I feel safe.

"Are you ready?" He asks.

"Well, I think so, Lord. All this is up to you."

"Very well," He says.

I sense clouds around us. I can't see them clearly, but I have to keep my eyes open to see anything at all.

[*Note: I hadn't experienced anything like this before. If I closed my eyes, I couldn't see anything in the Spirit either. I had to keep them open. It's like what I was seeing was superimposed over what my physical eyes were seeing. I also had to physically turn my head to look in other directions in the Spirit...*]

Jesus is still standing in front of me with His hands on my shoulders.

I hear sounds as in a jungle. The atmosphere seems a bit denser. There are some large leafed plants to either side of Jesus. I see something like a white snake slithering off to my left; it's about 5 feet long.

"He won't hurt you," Jesus says. I am aware of many more plants over to my left. I'm having to physically turn my heard left and right to look around and see other things.

Over to my right there are more plants, but there's a clear spot where I can see a high peaked mountain off in the distance. I thought I heard something behind me.

Again, I have to physically turn around...and there's a waterfall behind me. It's perhaps only about 6 feet high and a few feet behind me. I look down to see where the water is flowing. The stream is coming right at me... in fact I'm standing in it and didn't realize it!

I'm sitting back in my chair so I can type. It's almost like the chair is in the water. I can see the water flowing away from me towards Jesus. He's now standing about 15 feet in front of me. Strange, but I can't see the water going past Him. It seems to go to the base of his feet and disappears. I can hear the waterfall behind me with the burbling of water around me.

I am now aware of a couple large colorful birds... parrots, on either side of Jesus sitting in among the plants. I hear the sounds of other birds in the distance.

I hear a lion roaring somewhere off to my right and slightly behind me. I can now see her... it's a female maybe about 20 feet away. She's flicking her tail about. Jesus assures me again she won't hurt me.

I now see a very large tortoise (about 30 inches across) off to my left about 10 feet away. His neck is stretched out, but he's not moving much at all. I hear the lioness roaring again and glance over in her direction. She's much closer... and comes right up to me. I take my hand and stroke her head. She's like a big pussycat, purring and friendly. She takes one of her big paws and paws at my right arm, but not to hurt me. Her claws are partly extended, but they don't seem sharp. She seems very affectionate. (She's not as large as an African lion, rather more like a cougar, or mountain lion.)

I look over at the mountain again. It has the classic cone shape of a volcano and there seems to be a little smoke coming from the top.

I now look more intently to my left. The tortoise is still slightly out in front of me. However, straight to my left is that large, orange flower bud from my garden vision! I'm aware Jesus is smiling at me when I see it.

Do you want to know what it is?" He asks.

"Well, of course I do."

Jesus is grinning. "It's a surprise."

"Ok Lord, you already told me that." I think He's having some fun with me. (He definitely has a sense of humor...)

"Go smell it," He says.

I have to get out of my chair and go over to it. As I bend over it, it opens up. It looks different inside than the last time I saw it. Now it looks more like a giant tiger lily. I try smelling it, but all I can smell is the microwave popcorn I popped earlier in the kitchen! That physical smell seems to be overwhelming everything. I go back to my chair and sit down, but still looking at the flower.

Jesus says, "Go try smelling it again." I get back up and go over and try again. The physical smell of the popcorn is still the most noticeable thing. But in the spirit, I sense two smells mingled together somehow, oranges... and orange blossoms. It's not very prominent however.

Jesus says, "You will need to practice this. The more you practice seeing, listening, touching and smelling, the better you will become sensing these things."

I can readily hear the waterfall behind me. In fact, now that I'm listening, I can hear waves off to my right not far away.

"That's what this is Lord, isn't it? You said you were going to take me on a tour. It's a tour of the spiritual senses, isn't it?" Jesus is smiling and nods in the affirmative.

I spend some time just looking around. I see the white snake again, now over to my right out in front. It does not seem at all threatening.

I now also see what appears to be a stone birdbath over to my left just beyond the tortoise. It's no ordinary birdbath however, as there's water bubbling up in it. Some small birds like goldfinches have landed on the rim sipping water. Behind that is a palm tree. I'm familiar with a lot of palms, but I don't remember seeing any quite like this before. It's pinnate, with a very dark green super column, but only about 6-8 feet high. The spread is no more than 6-7 feet in diameter.

I now also hear wind in the trees. A few loose leaves fly about in the air.

I look up into the sky. I'm aware of huge area of radiant light overhead. It is not the sun, but I sense it's the light of God Himself. I wonder what's up there.

"Do you want to go look?" Jesus asks.

"Yes, Lord."
Jesus walks over towards me, places His hands on my shoulders again. "Are you ready?" He asks.

"Yes, Lord, I think I am."

I hear, "Close your eyes," so I do. It appears the vision is ending, as I'm not going any further at the moment...

Reflections afterwards:
After a bit I opened my eyes again and could feel the presence of the Lord around me. I assume He's got something else to show me during a future meeting.

Interestingly, even afterwards, I could still look around and see much of what I saw before. It's almost like another reality that's continuing on around me. Perhaps it's a place I can return to, much like the woodland garden.

At first, I was surprised to see the snake. We often associate them with evil, but the Lord created them along with all the other animals. So, like other animals, I suppose you can have good ones and bad ones. This snake did not seem at all threatening.

Something else I didn't record earlier; but while all this was going on, I thought I heard the Lord say these animals were there to serve me. That's interesting. I suspect there will be more about this vision to ponder...

Through The Door... Into Another Realm

I have finished reading reading a pre-release copy of "When Heaven Touches Earth." It is a scholarly paper co-written by Dr. Gary S. Greig, Dr. James W. Goll, Dr. Mark Virkler, Rev. Mike Rogers and Rev. Maurice Fuller. Its purpose is to give credence to — and place "heavenly encounters" into a clear Biblical perspective.

Mark Virkler also wrote the extraordinary course book, "How to Hear God's Voice," which I have also recently read. That has acted as the "ignition key" for my recent encounters.

I know Mike Rogers, who gave me this pre-release copy of "When Heaven Touches Earth." This book has really helped clarify and validate certain aspects of my recent experiences. I am privileged having received this copy.

A couple years ago in Brazil, I was in a service where Mike delivered the message. He led many into heavenly encounters that day. I myself had a vision of an old door. But I was afraid to pursue it. I told Mike afterwards, I was afraid — because it was an old door — it was leading to things of the past; things I was trying to let go of and set aside. Instead, I wanted to press on into the future. However, Mike encouraged me to go through it. He had the same experience and many, many other Christians around the world had seen the same, or a similar door. It was an invitation to visit heavenly places.

Since then I've seen the door (or similar door) many times. I've kept banging on it, wanting to go in. But nobody would open it. I was like a little child crying outside wanting to go in and see Daddy, but no one would open the door. I would continue crying, asking Daddy to please let me in...but to no avail.

Today, when nearing the end of the book, it was reinforced the Lord *wants* us to ascend to the throne room, where He can refresh us, provide encouragement and instruction for our task on earth. If this is true, there really should be no impediment to entering in. After all, Jesus has paid for the privilege.

As I finished reading this, a vision appeared...I saw the door. My attention was drawn to a large lever handle. OK, if the Lord really wants me to come through, I should be able to open this. I didn't bother knocking. Instead, I pushed down the lever and pushed open the door. The other side was full of light...everywhere. At first I couldn't see anything. But then I usually can't see in these visions very clearly anyway. Nonetheless, the Lord has been teaching me to keep looking...

I then became aware of an angel behind me, standing next to the door. He shut it behind me. None of this was very clear, but then it seemed there were two angels around me... ripping off of me what looked like dirty, old rotten clothing. I was then clothed in a white robe and what seemed like a small, golden band, or crown placed on my head.

When this short vision ended, I set the book aside for a break.

A bit later, I read the last appendix, which was written by Mike. It contained his brief teaching about meeting with the Lord in heaven. He finished it by sharing the first two encounters he personally experienced. The first told of his vision of the door while he was in prayer at a conference. Not knowing what Mike was experiencing, a man came up, placed his hand on Mike's shoulder and prophesied, "The Lord wants you to go through!" Mike then decided not to be passive, but to actively "press in." He began to push against the door with all his might, when it suddenly burst open. He described initially being flooded with light... and described what he subsequently saw.

Several things amazed me about this. First was his decision to be fully active and push the door open. I suddenly realized this had been part of my problem. I was waiting for someone else to open my door, but it was unlocked!! All I had to do was open it myself.

His initial experience of being flooded with light, was also identical with mine. The only difference was, he obviously had a vastly more vivid experience than I had. However, I think that will come in time as the Lord continues to train me and I continue to press into Him... exercising and learning to use my spiritual senses.

In the meantime, I continue to get flashes of this vision. I can readily go through the door... seemingly whenever I wish. I also continue to wear the white robe, even while entering. I can only assume the Lord has more to show me...

[After a short break, I returned to my chair and entered into prayer...]

"Ok Lord, is there something else you would like to show me here?"

I walk up to the door. I'm wearing my white robe. I push down the handle and open the door. Again I see a lot of light, but I also see a lot of beings here. Some of them have white robes and wings. There's a path opening up before me. It's like some kind of cobblestone but it's transparent and gray. I can see through it... I can see blue sky and a rainbow below. The pathway weaves through the sky into the distance, where there's some light ahead.
I'm at the beginning of the path with the door behind me. I seem to be standing in an area of solid ground that extends out about 15 feet in front of me. It almost looks like a cliff's edge ahead. The pathway goes up to the edge...and keeps on going straight ahead, right out into the air.

Although I'm only about 15 feet from the edge, the solid ground seems to stretch out an infinite distance to my right and left sides. I sense...and see many, many beings standing on both sides of me out into the distance, all standing on the solid ground. I see only a few winged beings flying to and fro in the air out in front in the distance. As I look further out into the distance, the path through the air seems to lead towards what might be a floating city surrounded by clouds. It looks like it could be several thousand feet away. The clouds surrounding the city are almost like wisps of fog... there's no top or bottom to them.

It's seems as if my presence is being noticed by all the beings around me. I can now hear what sounds like a lot of soft talking or murmuring.

Well, I'm this far, I might as well start walking down the path towards the city. As I start walking, I'm aware of an angel hovering about six feet away and slightly above my right side. I ask, "Who are you?" The reply, "I'm your guardian angel." I can tell he's smiling, but I can't make out any other details.

This is crazy, but it seems as if my robe is a bit too long. It's almost like I'm on the verge of tripping over it. I pick up the front to make walking easier. It seems as if we've covered the distance in almost no time. However, as I approach, I'm not seeing what I would have expected. I thought perhaps it was a city, but I was mistaken. Completely shrouded by the foggy clouds, the only way in is via the path. But there are no buildings inside. Instead it's full of massive, ugly, black, rocklike structures. Some of them tower hundreds of feet into the air, with only a suggested appearance of buildings. I don't like what I'm seeing. I'm having doubts if this is really of the Lord.

My angel says, "Let me take you." He and another angel lift me off of the path up into the air. I ask, "What is this I'm looking at?"

"It is all the rubbish removed from your life. It is being stored here to be thrown into the lake of fire with the devil and his angels and everything else that is unclean." You never have to come here again."

Suddenly I'm aware of an absolutely enormous area of light appearing to my upper left ahead.

The voice continues, "This is all to be left behind. The hurts, wounds, imperfections, everything that has hindered you. It has been purchased for the purpose of being discarded. You will never see it again."

My attention turns again towards the huge, brilliant area to my upper left. "Come, we will show you what you are about to receive... and then some." The angels are taking me in the air up higher towards the light. I can see a massive golden building surrounded by glowing, radiant cloud. I can't see much detail, but it appears to be a huge, golden city.

"Will I see more?"
"Yes, you will, but that is enough for now."

I'm placed back close to the door. As I look out again into the distance, the cobblestone pathway has burst into flames and is burning up. Bits of burning stuff drop down into the air and disappear. The path is eventually gone and the "refuse dump" is no longer accessible. The place containing all the rubbish is hardly visible, seems to be moving even further and fading away, displaced by the radiance of the glowing city.

All the beings on either side of me are now smiling at me. They start applauding and cheering. I'm really moved and tears come to my eyes.

The voice continues, "You can come back. Take a rest and contemplate what you have seen."

Everything seems to fade away, but as I now sit here in my chair it's as if a hidden reality has become even more real... just an arm's reach away...

Reflections afterwards:
When I saw the path leading into the distance, it took me by surprise. I would have expected it to have been made of gold. Instead, it was a rather drab, transparent gray color. The reason for this became apparent later...

The "cliff" edge as I described it, wasn't actually a cliff in an earthly sense. Yes, there was an edge, but it wasn't like an earthly cliff. You could peer out into the distance and over the edge, but I saw no visible land dropping off as with a cliff. Although it was an edge, what was beyond was simply sky and space both above and below. It was a demarcation of some kind.

Although I originally thought I saw what might be a glow coming from the supposed city, I now realize that area was not radiating light. Rather, it was being "highlighted" as an invitation for me to proceed towards it, which I did.

The multitude of beings on either side of me also seemed a bit strange, when I first saw them. I would have expected to see a lot of joyous activity, but instead it was as if they were just standing there, almost solemn...maybe waiting for something.

The appearance of my guardian angel was a surprise. I wondered why he would be needed there, other than perhaps as an escort. Of course, as things unfolded, it became apparent I was approaching an unclean place...and even walking on an unclean path. I suspect that's why I was almost tripping in my robe. It's as if even the pathway was constructed of things designed to "trip me up". The fact I couldn't see my guardian angel very clearly suggests my attention was not to be focused too much on him, but remain on my destination.

Actually, even at a distance, I could see the top of what looked like a "black building" poking up out from amongst the clouds. Again, I thought that odd, as I would have expected something like gold, but certainly not black. Because I was doubtful as to what I was seeing, I did not write that down at the time. The path could have easily been a couple thousand feet long. However, despite its length, it was as if we reached the other end almost instantly. As I approached the entrance of the place, the massiveness of the black, unclean "stuff" was stunning. I was just a speck in comparison to the size of all that stuff. How could that all fit in me? But then, perhaps it was also all the external junk surrounding, and imprisoning me, too. I don't think I even saw all of it. I certainly had no desire to spend any time looking at it. I never actually entered the area, I was only close enough to the entry point (maybe about 200 feet) so I could see into the area.

I found this statement interesting: All that black rubbish in my life had "been purchased for the purpose of being discarded." We know that Jesus purchased us. What we sometimes forget is, He purchased us, "as is," complete with all the rubbish. Because He owns us, he can choose what to keep and what to discard. Interesting... I've never thought of it quite that way before. And of course, his choosing is always perfect. He only throws away the bad stuff, though we might not recognize it as bad at the time.

The burning and destruction of the pathway was fascinating. The fact I was permitted to walk to... and see that place was interesting. However, all that rubbish is now completely cut off, inaccessible, reserved for eventual destruction. A path is a two-way street. I have to wonder if, in the spiritual realm, bits of that rubbish were still traveling back down that path into my life... or at least trying to. However, now it's clearly been cut off. Praise God!

The fact that all those heavenly beings were applauding and cheering afterwards really touched me and might suggest some kind of significant work was accomplished at that point. I don't yet have an answer for that, but I'm sure time will tell.

An Invitation

Throughout the day, I continue to see glimpses of the world beyond the door. Even while driving, suddenly there it is... in my mind's eye... just spontaneously popping up. I could now see a different pathway, a golden pathway meandering its way out into the air. It meanders its way somewhat more to the left...towards the massive glowing city in the distance. The "city of refuse" had previously been somewhat over to the right, but there's nothing of that to be seen.

Even though I was involved in my activities at work, I would stop momentarily to look into the vision. I had no idea something like this could occur simultaneously along with one's earthly activities also moving by. I sort of thought one must be quiet and waiting upon the Lord...and I'm certain that's when the most extended experience will occur. It's almost like this is an invitation. And I can't wait to go back.

At one point, I decided to take a closer look at this golden path. It was amazing and very hard to describe. It looked like it was made of small rounded blocks or stones, but was gold and transparent. I've heard of that before. However, what I saw next was unexpected. As I looked closer at the path... (this is so hard to describe) it looked like the stones were filled with golden liquid... (reminiscent of honey) that slowly undulated about. Within the currents were beautiful glistening, glowing ripples that glowed with bright, slowly undulating light. The golden walkway was glowing with undulating ripples of light, yet you could see through it.

I then became aware of two, bright white angels on either side of the pathway. I think they were waiting there to escort me.

So this evening, I wanted to spend some time with the Lord and see where this might lead. However, when I attempted to open my journal, the file was corrupted!

Alas, my evening was spent restoring the file, as I didn't want to lose anything. It's now late and I must retire, but I know where I want to go tomorrow!

An Opportunity Seemingly Lost

I can't believe it. Over a week has passed since I made it through the door, but I have yet to return. The next day or two I kept getting glimpses of my returning through the door, including the golden walkway.

I was set to return the next day when I discovered my journal file was corrupted. I spent a great deal of time getting it recovered. I obviously didn't want to lose anything.

Unfortunately, the next day ushered in another busy period. I've had so much going on...I wanted to have a time I could properly devote to going back through the door. However, it just never seemed like the right time. I was either too tired, too late...whatever. I now realize I've made the same mistake I made once before. When a vision presents itself, I really need to pursue it in short order. I can't believe I've done this again!!! Forgive me Lord...

I've been spending most of this evening with Lord. I've been rereading some of my journal entries again. Once again, the Lord has said so much, but I've been so dimwitted taking it to heart. I guess I would have fitted in with Jesus' disciples quite well in that respect...

I've haven't seen much this evening. It makes me sad, because I few days ago it was as if I was on the verge of exploring something new...

However, I have gotten glimpses of me opening the door again. So maybe there is something for me. Well, Lord Jesus, it's all up to you...

I can see the door. I'm wearing my white robe. I push down the handle and push the door open, but I'm not seeing anything past it. I'm hesitant to try to step through. If the Lord has nothing for me this evening, I don't want to force my way into anything.

I went back and read where I saw the golden pathway up close. I thought maybe it might lead to something opening up, but no. I'm really disappointed...and frustrated with myself too.

I keep looking, but it's as if there's a thin, black barrier of some kind immediately on the other side of the door casing. All I know is, I'm not going to force my way through that. Rather, I sense I just need to meditate on the Lord and let Him lead the way in whatever else I do with Him this evening...

Reflections about 4 weeks later:
I now believe the thin black barrier was a trick of the enemy. The Lord does not take His good gifts back away from us. In hindsight, it's now obvious with all the distractions going on for many days, the enemy did not want me going back through the door.

The fact is, if I've placed myself wholeheartedly in the Lord's hands, what could happen to me? It's true, there is such a thing as a lost opportunity. I've learned that. However, would the Lord allow me to see the door, open it and then allow something bad happen to me? What loving parent would set a trap just inside the door of their house, to injure their children when they come home from school? Completely ridiculous.

The problem was, I got focused on the unexpected, black barrier. I don't remember specifically asking the Lord anything about it. Instead, I simply *assumed* He didn't want me going through. If something like this ever happens again, I won't rely on just what I think I'm seeing or understand. I need to specifically ask the Lord and keep my trust in Him.

A Frank Talk with Jesus—
In an Unexpected Place

I was rereading through previous journal entries. I haven't had any visions in days. I have however been pursuing the Lord and finished going through all 480 scripture references in Mark Virkler's book regarding seeing in the Spirit.

I was reading an earlier encounter and started seeing a lot of stuff swirling around me.

"OK, Lord, is there something you wish to show me here?"

I am aware of a lot of wind blowing. I can hear it and get glimpses of things blowing around and past me. I see dead leaves being caught up in the wind, swirling around. It seems like a dark area. I now see Jesus standing out in front of me, his arms beckoning. The wind is making a lot of noise and we're surrounded by a lot of darkness. Other than Jesus, I can't see much of anything.

"Lord, I'm here, but I'm not sure what's going on."

He smiles, "I just want you to talk to me."

"Ok Lord. This vision thing has had me on a bit of a roller coaster. I read back over earlier entries and they are really valuable. I'm also struck by how slow I am to respond to things. Even when I think a vision is perhaps coming, I confess to a certain amount of fear and hesitancy. I'm afraid of making mistakes, of missing you. There's also a bit of fear of the unknown. A few of these visions have gone down some strange paths, so when they were occurring, I questioned them. I think that has bred some fear...uncertainty.

"Have I misled you, so far?" Jesus asks.

"No, Lord, it's actually been exciting in retrospect. But for some reason I keep thinking I'm going to have some bizarre experience that's not of you. However, I was recently reading in Ezekiel and Daniel. They had some extraordinary visions that not only defied their understanding, but the understanding of many to follow. Yet, your truth stands, and the Body has recognized your truth in these visions, though not everything is yet thoroughly understood.

So, Lord, I guess I need to reach out and trust you no matter what happens.
I repent of my reluctance and fear. But I also admit needing your help in this area, Lord."

"I will," he says.

"So Lord, I just want to state here and now, I'll try to the best of my ability to hang on for the ride. I want to continue walking with You. I'm willing to accept whatever it is you have waiting for me."

I continue to see Jesus standing there, arms outstretched towards me. I run up to Him and hug Him.

"Forgive me for my failures. I do want to learn."

"Oh, you are forgiven, indeed," he says with a smile.

I continue to hug Him and don't want to let go. The area around us is dark and windy.

"What is this place Lord?"

"It is a place of your own making. It is not where I want you to be. I have come to deliver you from this place. We must dismantle the lies and treachery of the enemy. I will heal and deliver you."

I continue to see Jesus, but no more darkness as the vision fades.

I sense I need to cooperate with Jesus in this. He said, "*We* must dismantle..." In other words, I need to be involved, engaged.

Reflections afterwards...

"A place of my own making." Wow. How do we make such places? A few might be:
- Believing the lies of enemy instead of believing God...
- Trusting in ourselves instead of trusting in Him...
- Not appropriating what He has given us...
- And undoubtedly many other things!

Some of what the prophets saw in their visions left them distressed. I can still get glimpses of the darkness with the dead leaves blowing about. I suspect the Lord will be bringing things to my attention in the coming days. I pray I have the sensitivity to pounce on these matters as soon as He reveals them...and see what part I have to play in seeing these matters taken care of.

When Jesus said, "A place of your own making," I sensed it was a statement of fact, not condemnation. In fact, I sensed no condemnation, but the place didn't feel very nice.

He went on to mention the dismantling of "the lies and treachery of the enemy." I've been contemplating this and am reminded of Adam and Eve in the garden. Although they created problems for themselves by their bad choices, they made those choices because they were deceived.

Undoubtedly, some of the discomfort I've felt in myself is a result of my own choices and beliefs buried deep inside. However, these were the result of deception crafted by the enemy. I have been at least partially aware of some of these issues, but have never been able to fully "get a handle" on them. Even after receiving much ministry over the years, some issues remain seemingly hidden and intractable.

However, the Lord has promised to deliver me and I cling to that promise. I am reminded of when the Israelites seemingly faced an insurmountable problem: Pharaoh's army trapping them on one side, with the sea on the other. However, Moses said, "Do not be afraid. Stand firm and you will see the deliverance the Lord will bring you today. The Egyptians you see today you will never see again. The Lord will fight for you; you need only to be still."

I was really moved looking at that passage again. Though the Israelites were helpless in themselves, they did have one part to play. *God provided the miraculous pathway of deliverance – but they had to choose to walk down the path.*

Jesus Versus the Enemy — No Contest!

I was again studying previous encounters in my journal...

I've been seeing glimpses of a dragon...

I see a large dragon. It's roaring and bellowing out fire. It stomps about, seemingly ferocious, but looks frequently upwards and blows fire into the sky...this way and that way. Now it seems to be getting frantic... and continues to blow fire upwards. I see two giant hands reach down from above...the dragon now seems small in comparison. The arms seemingly extend out of sleeves from a white robe. The giant hands grab hold of the dragon and twist the body, much like one might wring the neck of a chicken. The dragon, which is small in comparison, is tossed down and lies limp, dead on the ground.

I begin to see more...an area above the arms is unveiled... it's Jesus. His face is full of tender compassion as he looks at me. The detail I can see is limited, but his eyes are so compassionate.

"It's easy for me," he says. "When you first saw the dragon it looked so big, ferocious and noisy. But for me, it was effortless to dispose of. So it will be with the problems you have faced. Hurts, wounds; all will be cast down as the dragon."

Jesus seems so big. I'm scooped up in his hands... I'm in his hands and light seems to emanate from them. His compassionate face is still looking at me. I'm in a state of wonderment as Jesus is soooo big! I've never seen him this way before.

"I am so much more than your problems," He says.

"Wow Lord, I hardly know what to say. You're SO big...so awesome!"

Jesus seems to be getting even bigger...and bigger...I am surrounded by his huge hands. What could possibly ever harm me here? Nothing...it's impossible. Jesus is so much more than anything we can imagine. It's like, He appears to us, and yet at the same time He fills the universe.

"Is there anything else here Lord, you would like to show me?"

I'm in His hands, but can look out and see the earth below, stars, planets...
"It is a playground for my children," he says. "There is much prepared for you."

"Wow, when can I start to enjoy all this Lord?"

"Sooner than you think..." He replies.

I sense there is SO much He has prepared for us. And it's ready to be explored even now...with Him as our guide.

The vision doesn't seem to be going anywhere further at the moment. The last image, looking out into the universe is still with me. Jesus is SO big, He fills it all, yet He holds me safely in the palms of his hands. And He's prepared it all for us!

Reflections afterwards:
It's interesting how the vision started with the focus on the dragon. But in the end, there was no more thought of it...completely out of mind. The only remaining thing was the overwhelming magnificence of Jesus, His love, and what He has prepared for us.

My First Visit into The Throne Room

I've been getting glimpses of a huge golden throne...a golden city in the clouds...

I'm back at the cliff edge, two angels in white are there, one on each side of a golden path. It's the same golden path I saw once before. It's somewhat transparent. The paving blocks look as if they are filled with golden honey and glowing light that glistens and moves about. With an angel on each side, they take me by the arms and we walk forward onto the golden path. It almost feels alive under my feet...like life is radiating from it.

I take a few steps forward. It's like I'm entering a world of life and leaving a world of darkness and death behind. I step out a bit further. I can see the golden path weaving through the sky out to the golden city in the clouds in the distance. Interestingly, I instinctively seem to know it's not necessary to walk the whole distance. Just thinking about it... and suddenly I'm well along the path close to the city.

The city is like the sun in the clouds, but as the sun is just a small spot of light, this is a huge, radiating area in the clouds.

"Come, let's go closer," the angels say. I'm now at what looks like a massive glowing gate reaching into the sky. It's two halves open up and swing open. Oddly, the one on the left swings in and the one on the right swings out. Light is everywhere inside.

I think there is much more to see, but I've been transferred directly into the giant throne room. I can sort of make out walls behind me, but not out in front. It seems to go out forever. There is a huge throne before me. I can't really judge its size, but maybe at least 50 feet high...maybe bigger. Its form does not appear to be particularly ornate. It appears to be sitting on pavement that is like a transparent aqua color.

A huge area of light is in the center of the throne.

I suddenly find myself up on the throne, with a massive area of soft, warm light around...almost enveloping me. Two giant hands appear out of the light and set me...in a lap. It's hard to explain, but I know I'm sitting in the Lord's lap. I can look out and see a few doors in the distance in the back of the room, but they seem very small from this vantage point. There are also some heavenly beings standing there.

"Lord, I've always wanted to sit in your lap."

"You are always welcome here. I paid a dear price to get you here."

I feel like a little child in this place.

Suddenly it all seems to dissolve and I'm back with my angels at the beginning of the path. I think it's all I could handle for the moment...

Reflections some days later:
This vision transpired rather quickly and my visit was brief. There was probably a contributing factor to that. Because my visions so far have not approached anything like an out of body experience (such as Paul shared, and some people today have experienced), I remain very much aware of my physical surroundings. This is actually typical of most people's experiences. With this in mind, Mark Virkler recommends being in a comfortable position and in a comfortable place, free of distractions...as one normally would be during prayer.

Though much rarer, if someone enters a trance (as Peter did when he saw the sheet with unclean animals being lowered from heaven), or is potentially out of the body (as Paul shared), one apparently becomes oblivious to their physical surroundings.

However, as is typical during most prayer, we are normally quite cognizant of our surroundings. In this situation, it was a hot day and my leather chair was becoming uncomfortably sticky. I think subconsciously, I was hoping the vision wouldn't last too long, because of my increasing discomfort and desire to leave my chair. And because of this, it was brief.

It was a lesson in not only devoting quality time to prayer, but the necessity to deal with distractions...hopefully ahead of time. It's all part of being prepared and giving our wholehearted best to the Lord.

A Lesson in God's Personality

I was re-reading some encounters some have shared in the book, *"When Heaven Touches Earth."* I came across one, where a lady was sharing her journey through inner healing. She made this statement, which captured my attention: "I believed I was a mistake, not really part of my family growing up; I played the role of onlooker. I had imaginary friends. I didn't believe anyone would ever want me as friend, wife, etc..."

Though not an exact description of myself, certain facets nonetheless caught my attention, especially when she said, "I believed I was a mistake." As an adult, I've never considered myself a mistake. But the Spirit has reminded me of something I did ponder when I was young.

I wasn't like many of the other boys. I didn't like rough-and-tumble games. I had a low tolerance for pain, was hurt easily and didn't like rough, noisy, boisterous activities. Rather, I appreciated quiet, gentle activities. I had a sensitive, artistic side that loved color, music and nature. Therefore, items often intended for boys such as sporting equipment and toy guns had no appeal to me whatsoever. Rather, I had more appreciation for things that supposedly "only girls liked."

Even at an early age I became aware of this. The attitudes sometimes voiced by my family and classmates only reinforced this perception...and did so repeatedly.

My classmates often, and cruelly compared my lack of physical coordination to a girl.

One time when ice skating, my frustrated father said in disgust, "You skate like a girl..."

I was over at a friend's house where his mother made us grilled cheese sandwiches. I proceeded to slice mine in half as it was neater to eat. She responded, "What *boy* cuts his sandwich in half?"

I became friends with a boy from another class at school. He liked science, just like I did. We did a lot of things together for some months. However, suddenly he wouldn't return my phone calls. Finally, after repeated attempts, his parents got him on the phone. He told me, "Please don't call anymore. My mom doesn't want me playing with you anymore. She says you act too much like a girl." I hung up the phone utterly devastated.

These are but a very few examples.

At one point as a child, I remember wondering if indeed, I was some kind of mistake. Perhaps I was really intended to be a girl...but something went wrong.

"Lord, as a child, I wondered if I was a mistake. What would you like to tell me about this?"

"You still wonder. But it's untrue. I made you exactly as you are. I have given you qualities that many men do not have or understand. Yet, I understand, because they come from Me. They are a part of who I am too. You are a reflection of who I am."

"We made man in Our image." *[This was spoken very powerfully, almost like plural voices.]*

"Societies have twisted who I am and have twisted many who I've created. No one man can reflect in entirety who I am. Each is a partial reflection, but when all put together, reflect Me in My entirety. This is why I inspired Paul to write about the importance of the body to the Corinthian church. Each member is a reflection of Myself, but only in part. But when all the parts work harmoniously together, they reflect the completeness of harmony between Myself, the Father and the Holy Spirit.

Yes, what I made was corrupted by your upbringing, but we are fixing that. I have come to restore and heal you."

"Lord, forgive me for doubting the wisdom of your creation, because unknowingly, that's what I was doing. I just didn't know any better."

Jesus continues, "I don't want you to shun who you are, but to grow in it. Everything I have given you is Good. Embrace Me, because as you do, you will embrace yourself as well. You will come to see yourself, as I do."

Later Reflections:
All the incidents mentioned above (plus many, many others) have been ministered into over the years. Furthermore, as an adult, I've intellectually known these truths for some time.

However, when reading the testimony out of that book, I was reminded that as a child, I did indeed wonder if I was a mistake. The child in me still wondered...and still needed affirmation.

I've since had several visions of myself as a child in Jesus' lap, receiving His loving acceptance. It does appear a new peace has settled into an old, dark corner of my past that I had forgotten was there.

Interestingly, I had a sense it was not only just Jesus speaking. For example, when that phrase came forth: "We made man in Our image," it was as if the Godhead in unison was speaking...as One. Much of the time, it was as if Jesus was the mouthpiece, but during that one statement, there was a strong, palpable sense of the Godhead speaking in unison. Amazing.

However, when He said, "Yes, what I made was corrupted by your upbringing, but we are fixing that," — the "we" is referring to the Lord and myself together. It was an interesting phrase, "we are fixing that." I had the distinct impression He was referring to a cooperative effort. The Lord, of course, does the healing, but I need to cooperate and act upon what He is showing me. I must be in agreement, and be engaged with what He wishes to do.

One thing that gave me pause was when He said, *"No one man can reflect in entirety who I am. Each is a partial reflection, but when all put together, reflect Me in My entirety."* At first, I wondered about this. How can even all the humans who've ever existed reflect God in His entirety? After all, He is limitless. Even all the people who've ever existed are still a finite number. However, what follows sheds some light on this: *"This is why I inspired Paul to write about the importance of the body to the Corinthian church. Each member is a reflection of Myself, but only in part. But when all the parts work harmoniously together, they reflect the completeness of harmony between Myself, the Father and the Holy Spirit."*

There are many types of gifting and talents, but also many types of personalities. Psychologists have attempted to identify personality types by noting obvious differences in people such as:

- Those who "feel" versus those who "reason."
- Those who "rely on their senses" versus those who "rely on intuition."
- "Introverts" versus "extroverts," etc.

It's true that all of humankind put together cannot truly reflect all that God is. Even the entire universe can't do that. However, when it comes to *personality*, the scriptures tell us, "God made man in His image." Therefore, if we look at all the different personalities distributed across mankind, God's personality is all of these "types and varieties" integrated together in perfect harmony.

That's why if we try to shoehorn God's personality into just "a certain type", we come away with a mistaken idea of who He really is. Some have thought of God as a stern judge waiting to strike us down. Others have painted Him as a loving God who loves us so much, he couldn't possibly send anyone to hell. Both of these are distorted views of who God really is, because they focus only on specific characteristics of His personality to the exclusion of others.

Light Dispelling the Darkness

I can hear the wind swirling around me. A few leaves blow around in the swirls of air. I think I'm back in the same place I was before; the dark place Jesus said was of my own making.

Jesus is out in front of me with His arms open toward me. However, the place has changed. There's light breaking through now behind Jesus. It's breaking through dark clouds in the sky. Oddly, though this light is coming from behind Jesus, His front side facing me is fully lit. I can see His hair...it kind of wavy, dark, but with some brown in it.

The atmosphere is somehow different.

I am aware of a river meandering through a valley below, with mountains in the distance. I can hear wind blowing through what sounds like fir trees behind me, but I don't seem permitted to look behind me at the moment.

"Come", Jesus says. I walk towards Him. He takes me to the edge of the high area where we are standing. I can see more of the valley below.

"Lord, is this the place we were before?"

"Yes and no. The dark place you were in before was not as large as you thought. Even now I am cleaning the darkness away. There is much I have prepared for you, but the darkness was obscuring it."

I can see some black rocks scattered about on the ground. Some of them tumble over the edge of the high place where we are standing. I can see some on the slope down in front of me. However, the valley below is beautiful green. Nonetheless, there are some dark clouds around and I sense there's some dirty stuff floating in the water down below.

"Just a small work has opened this up to you," Jesus says. "There is more to be cleaned up, but have no fear, I will make it all clean. I am not yet finished. As you are purified, you will see more and more, new vistas like this will open before your eyes."

I have a feeling He's speaking somewhat allegorically.

"Yes, you will be purified. It will take some time, but not as much time as you might think. Remember, my time scale is different than yours. What seems to take a long time to you goes very quickly in my world."

"Lord, I assume these dark rocks, the dark clouds the stuff in the water below represents junk in my life that still needs to be taken care of."

Jesus nods in the affirmative.

"Just the one little work performed the other day has transformed what looked like total darkness into what you see before you. There is a great deal of beauty here, though there is still work to be done. Again, have no fear, it will be accomplished."

Jesus raises His arms higher. "Be at peace. You have much to experience. I will not give you more than you can handle. Continue to meditate on our experiences together. You will learn even from that. And I will open even more doors of revelation to you."

He now raises his arms high into the sky and looks up. "Bless him Father as you have blessed me."

Reflections afterwards:
The narrative above doesn't fully reflect everything that was happening. I tried to write down as best I could as it happened. Some things were unveiled faster than I could write them down. That's one reason I write these reflections afterwards; to fill in the gaps, so to speak.

When I asked if we were back in the same place, Jesus replied, "Yes and no". I didn't get it written at that moment, but it was if He was saying: "Yes it's the same place, but I'm in the process of rebuilding it."

I could see the black rocks around from the very beginning of the vision and sensed what they represented, but it took a while before I could get the question out.

Two statements Jesus made:
"Just a small work has opened this up to you..."
"Just the one little work performed the other day has transformed what looked like total darkness into what you see before you..."

He's referring to the previous vision, when He reminded me that as a child, I had questioned whether I was a mistake. Something definitive has been healed in this area. As an adult, I've never considered myself a mistake, however, something to this effect was apparently still buried deep inside. During the hours that followed that experience, I could recite, "I am no mistake," and witness something deep inside had genuinely changed. I could say it with a new, very deep conviction. I would have the say this truth has permeated through to the core of my being.

So, what Jesus was saying is, this "small work" has produced significant impact resulting in my eyes being opened to new things. There is still some clutter left, but He assured me the work would be entirely finished.

The blessing at the end is mind blowing: "Bless him Father as you have blessed me."

That the Father would bless me in the same way He blessed Jesus?? When you stop and think about what that entails, it's incredible. It seems inconceivable, yet it is Biblically harmonious. That's why Jesus came and died for us...so we could share in His blessings. Beyond amazing...

An Encounter with The Father

I was taking an evening shower and talking with the Lord. I was thinking about some of the places He's taken me earlier this year. I was reminded, He often told me I could come back to some of those places. Though this is true, any return visits so far have been primarily at His instigation. It was then I heard in my spirit, I could choose any place to revisit now and He would take me there. After a moment of thought I chose to revisit the throne room and visit the Father...

I see Jesus' hands stretching towards me. I take them and hold on firmly. I can now begin to see Him as He is smiling at me.

"Are you ready?" He asks.

"Well, yes, I guess so, Lord."

"You guess so?" He asks.

"Yes Lord, please, yes I'm ready..."

A wind suddenly swirls around us. Odd, again as in some previous visions I see some dead leaves swirling around, but then a light appears behind Jesus. The light comes toward and over us and feels warm. It's as if the light is part of the wind as it blows past us.

"Are you ready?" Jesus asks again.

"Yes Lord."

The wind continues to blow. I don't see dead leaves anymore, but sparkles of light swirling around in the wind.

Suddenly light appears below us. I see what appears to be gold pavement under our feet right in the area where we are standing. Around us there's a mist covering the ground, but it seems to be rolling back uncovering more of the pavement. The pavement is glowing with light, but gold also.

I see a throne in the distance. Suddenly it's in front of me. I see Jesus sitting on the throne. But then I'm aware of a much larger throne appearing behind ...it's as if it's being unveiled to me. It's much, much larger. Jesus now stands up from His throne and presents me to the Father. I see a huge light and some features of a face smiling at me.

"Come," a deep voice says. It sounds like plural voices together.

"I have brought him to you, Father." Jesus is smiling.

"Come my son," the Father says to me.

I find myself in the Father's lap. It's warm and full of soft light. I look out and see Jesus out in front smiling at me.

"What would you like?" the Father asks me.

"Like? To know you better, Lord. To be whole in You. To know your heart. Lord, I want to see you everywhere as I walk through the day. I want to be acutely aware of your presence. I just want to walk in step with you."

"And so you shall," He says. "And so you shall."

"My son will teach you. He has all knowledge. He knows everything about me. He will lead you to me just as He has led you here today."

"Father, I missed having an earthly father. I don't know what that's like. There are voids that need to be filled." Jesus smiles as I say this.

"My Son will fill those too. There isn't anything He can't do. Ask Him."

"Lord Jesus, as much as it is possible, can you lead me into a knowledge of the Father, just like You have? I desperately need to know Him and You."

"And when you know Me, you will know Him also," Jesus says. "I and the Father are one."

I'm now back, out in front of the throne with Jesus standing in front and the glory of the Father behind Him. Jesus raises his arms... and as He does, I also see huge images of arms rising behind Him.

"We will make our dwelling within you," I hear the plural voices saying.

I'm now standing in front of Jesus, His arms on my shoulders. He's smiling at me.
"I will help you, and indeed am helping you. Your desire to know the Father is pure, like that of a little child. I will honor you for that."

"Honor me?" I ask. "I don't understand."

Jesus laughs, "You don't need to understand that now. I love you and am blessing you. The trials and tribulations you are experiencing are from me. They are a test. You have decisions to make. This will strengthen you. Don't forget, I'm always at your side, even at these frustrating times."

The vision seems to be ending for the moment.

Reflections afterwards:
Sometimes knowledge is imparted to me that might not be understood by simply reading what I wrote at the time of the experience. When Jesus said, *"The trials and tribulations you are experiencing are from me,"* He was not referring to evil things done to me during the course of life — indeed He abhors such things. Rather, He was speaking of the challenges of life, such as meeting financial needs, dealing with relational issues etc. When we are buffeted by such circumstances, we have choices to make. We can either choose to seek the Lord and His ways...or worldly answers, which often lead to destruction.

I had a sense the dead leaves I initially saw swirling about represented impurities in my life...and perhaps my surroundings as well. However, these could not remain in the presence of the divine wind and light that enveloped us.

As I saw Jesus sitting on His throne, I then saw the much larger one coming into view, being unveiled behind Jesus. It was somewhat to my left and behind. Initially that had me concerned because that means Jesus was somewhat to the left of the Father, where the scriptures describe Him as being seated at the Father's right hand. However, I began to understand what was happening. The primary emphasis in the vision was the unveiling of the Father with Jesus being between us.

As Jesus stood and subsequently presented me to the Father, Jesus' throne was not even in view anymore. Instead, He was standing between the Father and myself. The only time this was not the case, was the brief time I spent in the Father's lap.

After that, Jesus was again in front of me with the Father behind. The oneness of Jesus and the Father was emphasized, especially when Jesus raised His hands, and the giant image of the Father's hands going up at the same time. Jesus is the go-between. Knowing Him is to know the Father (John 14:9, "Anyone who has seen me has seen the father.")

In particular, seeing Jesus between me and the Father also reminded me of Colossians 1:15, "The Son is the image of the invisible God..." and John 12:45, "The one who looks at me is seeing the one who sent me."

Jesus being one with the Father, yet separate...it's all beyond our understanding. All I know is I want and need to keep pursuing Him...

Preparing for an Encounter

[Note: This journal entry does not contain a vision experience, but rather was preparatory in nature. I had been seeing glimpses of Jesus at a banquet table and knew something was coming. I had a sense He was going to use the time of Christmas to do something with — and in me. But I also felt led to write down the following narrative, concerning how Christmas time affects me. I had a feeling it was to set the stage for what was to follow, whatever that might be.]

Christmas Eve…

Every Christmas since moving to the UK, someone has invited me over for Christmas dinner. However, this year that didn't happen.

Christmas time for me is invariably a bittersweet time. Memories surface from my early childhood Christmas times. Those Christmases were a time of wonderment, happiness and excitement. In contrast, most of the time one could not describe our home as happy place. My father had drinking problems, a violent temper and other issues intruded from our extended family. However, my mother did a remarkable job of shielding my brother and I from those unpleasantries. She succeeded admirably while we were still young. In particular, memories of our early Christmases were bright spots in the midst of the often-repressive, dark atmosphere in our home.

Fifty years ago this year, my grandmother, whom I was very close to, suddenly died at age fifty-nine of a heart attack. Brought on by simultaneous addictions to alcohol, cigarettes and prescription drugs, this occurred just two weeks before Christmas. It was the most traumatic experience of my life. I was only twelve years old and didn't know the Lord at that time. I was utterly devastated. The searing, unbearable pain of utter loss and agony pierced to the innermost parts of my very being and left me wounded for years.

My mother could no longer shield my brother and I from what was happening. In effect, the innocence of my childhood was torn from me that year. And I wasn't ready to have it taken away. My grandfather, suffering from loss, also became enslaved to the bottle. My father's drinking worsened. My poor mother, caught up in all this was deeply affected herself. And everything was now laid open for my brother and I to experience.

During the next three years, numerous other events from within my family and at school conspired to crush my spirit, leaving me depressed, sorrowful and embittered. My mother eventually faced having to choose between the lesser of two evils: Was it better for her two boys to have a really bad father at home…or no father at all? But then a critical event occurred where she realized there was no choice. She had to divorce my father. Thus, our already dysfunctional family further disintegrated…if that was even possible. A few years later, my ailing father passed away at only 47 years old.

Much has happened since then. Starting the very year of my father's passing, the Lord began to minister glorious inner healing into my soul. That same year, my mother happily remarried and was taken in by her husband's family. My brother also married that same year and found himself in a new family. However, for me marriage seemed like an abstract concept…something that even up to the present just doesn't seem meant to be.

Over my adult years, life's circumstances have kept me thousands of miles from my brother's family and my mother. So in a sense, I have inwardly felt orphaned.

However, I've never been totally alone. Since coming to the Lord in my college years, He has given me many good friends. These have been immensely appreciated. Over the years my friends have watched out for me and especially during the holidays, have kept me in mind.

As mentioned, Christmas in particular is a bittersweet time. Happy memories from my early childhood are on one hand, but memories of deep hurt and loss on the other. Getting together with friends at Christmas has always helped reinforce the positive memories, though the sorrowful ones were always lurking, never far away.

This Christmas, for the first time in many decades, I find myself alone. But I know I'm not really alone. The Lord always seems to do little things to remind me of His presence. A few days ago, I found myself somewhat depressed at facing Christmas alone. However, I was talking to the Lord about it and quoted to Him the scripture, "God sets the lonely in families… (Psalm 68:6) I was claiming this truth and told Him I really could use some encouragement.

The very next day after church, a family unexpectedly asked me over for dinner. I was treated to an absolutely marvelous, home cooked meal and a wonderful time of visiting. It dramatically lifted my spirits and although Christmas was a few days away, it was almost like a Christmas dinner to me. I was filled with peace, encouragement and looking forward to spending Christmas with the Lord.

For the past couple days, I've been getting glimpses of the Lord sitting at the head of a very long banquet table… It is now well past my bedtime, but perhaps tomorrow I'll find out what this is about.

An Encounter with The Holy Spirit

Christmas Day, in the evening...

I've gone through the door I've seen in previous visions. The foreground, up to the edge of the cliff is very dark. Beyond the edge of the cliff, everything is brilliant. The sky is resplendent with light...I see the golden path leading somewhat to the left out into the expanse of brilliant sky towards the golden city, alive with light. There are some winged angels flying about in the distance. I am then aware of two angels on either side of me beckoning me forward. I am dressed in my white robe. As I look down, I also seem to be wearing some kind of white shoes, though I cannot see them clearly. It's strange how the ground around me is dark, almost black, but everything beyond the cliff edge is brilliant with light. The angels, one on the left, the other on the right, take my arms and lead me forward. I'm transported out along the pathway and up to the city entrance in mere moments. I look back and can see where I entered...it almost looks like a black hole in the distance. I look forward and see the towering gates before me. As they open, there is blinding light emanating from within. The light is almost alive and pleasantly warm. The angels usher me forward into the light and I'm overwhelmed by it. As I stand in the light, I also feel a breeze blowing over me. It's as if black bits of something—almost like small pieces of black tissue paper—are being blown off my skin. [*Note:* These were coming off me, not my robe, which was clean and white.] They disappear behind me and vanish.

I continue to stand in the light and breeze. It's almost like the breath of God Himself is blowing over me. I look down and see my robe glowing brighter. I see a face in the light smiling at me.

"I just want to stay in your presence Lord."

As I continue to stand there basking in the light, I start to inhale and taking in the breeze. Suddenly, something like a black snake is expelled out of my right side. A hand reaches out of the light and grabs it. The hand continues to hold it out in front of me off to my right.

"What is that Lord?"

"It has been torturing you and I will no longer permit it." I begin to see the form of the Lord. He's holding the snake, bending it sharply over in half within His hand. It seems powerless and doesn't even struggle.

"Do you want me to get rid of it?" He asks.

"Of course Lord," I respond.

"Then you must release it as well," He says.

"How am I to do that, Lord? What is it?"

"It was planted in you as a child. It wants to depress and immobilize you. But you continue to hold onto it."

I'm quite perplexed.

"You are holding on to things of the past. I have prepared a glorious future for you, but you must be willing to release that which happened long ago."

"I am willing to do that Lord," I respond. Without a moment's hesitation, he squeezes the snake — it pops and vanishes.

"There. That was simple," Jesus says.

I stand in wonderment, bewildered.

"It is right to remember the past, but in a proper perspective. You didn't know it then, but I was always with you, always protecting you. The enemy would like to destroy you, but I have not permitted it."

"As you continue to seek me, we will redeem the past. Yes, that which hurt you will be turned into something glorious. There is nothing I cannot turn into glory, but you have to be willing to give it up, seek and continue to be bathed in My peace. In my peace you will find healing and contentment. In my peace you will find wholeness."

"Lord, what was the banquet table I kept seeing?"

"It is an invitation, and you will soon experience it. Keep seeking Me."

The warm breeze and light is blowing over me again. It's as if stuff keeps peeling away from me. It's almost like my skin becomes paper thin as the breeze blows in, through and around me.

Suddenly I find myself back standing by the door, looking back out in the direction of the golden city. Though the general area on this side of the cliff edge is still quite dark, the area around me is no longer black, but is being illuminated…by me! I look down in astonishment…I'm glowing…light is coming out from me and illuminating the dark area around me.

"Go now; you will come back." You will take my light with you and illuminate those around you. I love you. Go in peace…and I will always be with you."

I come back through the door, but am aware I can go back whenever I need to.

Later reflections:
I actually continued into the vision of the banquet table only a few minutes after the above ended. However, I've felt appropriate to insert some comments at this point, as they pertain specifically to the above.

Two evenings after this vision, I was attending a small worship meeting with some friends. During worship, I found myself again on the golden walkway with the manifest presence of God before me. The "breeze" — the breath of God was again blowing over me. Once more, it was if it was both blowing in, around and through me at the same time. It was as if I was almost "transparent" to the breeze.

I became aware that the breeze was the Spirit of God...flowing around and through me. As I pondered this, the words "flowing around me" suddenly came to my attention. I was reminded of the earlier vision: "A Lesson in God's Provision."

In that vision I saw a little bird flying about, carefree, landing in a stream, taking a sip of water and continuing his flight. Jesus went on to say (with italics I now just added):

> "Did he have to spend a lot of time looking for this water?" Jesus asks. "No *it's all around him*. All he had to do was land in it, take a sip and off he went. He didn't have to spend a great deal of time searching for it. It's here in abundance for him."

> "So it is with my provision in your life. It's not far away. *It's flowing all around you.* You just need to stop, let it flow around you and take a sip. Take as much as you need, because it is inexhaustible."

After that experience I wrote:

> "So when first hearing this, my natural inclination was to think in terms of financial provision. However, I sensed in my spirit, that was not the focus here, but rather the Lord was referring primarily to spiritual provision. After all, everything connected to our well-being originates in the spirit, not the flesh. Everything flows out from the spirit."

Suddenly all this was coming together. Regarding God's provision in my life, it's not so much *it* is flowing around me, but *He*, (the Holy Spirit) is flowing around me. As I previously noted, "Everything flows out from the spirit," but now I need to capitalize "Spirit." Before I was thinking in general terms—all of reality actually originates in the spiritual realm (see Hebrews 11:3). However, more specifically, everything originates from Him, the Holy Spirit.

The fact is, to experience God's provision, I don't need to dip into *it*, but rather "dip" into *Him*, the Holy Spirit, who is the source of all provision. We need to "stop," take a break from our busy lives and let Him flow in, around and through us.

I now realize the river flowing around me in that vision was the Holy Spirit. I now will have to go back and examine where water appeared in my earlier visions…as this may pertain to the Spirit as well. Offhand, I remember the vision at the beach — how the water was flowing around my hands and the grains of sand. Jesus himself identified that as the Spirit. Then there was the woodland garden with the bubbling spring… I can see I will have much to review and ponder about these matters…

A few additional observations pertaining to what I saw:
The fact the area on the other side of the door was dark up to the cliff edge was interesting. The door itself seems like a portal into the spiritual realm. The area immediately beyond, though part of the spiritual realm, seems as if it is somehow connected or associated with the physical realm, but clearly separate from Heaven beyond.

Interestingly, Paul talks about being caught up into "the third heaven," suggesting different levels of existence within the spiritual realm. Some have speculated the first heaven refers to the sky above, which is actually part of the physical realm. The second heaven would be just beyond into the spiritual realm where spirits of various kinds, including demons can move about. The third heaven would be where God "dwells" — a place of supreme holiness and purity where nothing unclean exists.

People who've had near death or out of body experiences talk about being in a place where they can still see what's happening on earth, but that place being clearly separate from Heaven. In some instances, people have shared being ushered through, past that lower realm into Heaven beyond…and then back. In the book, "Heaven Is Real," the little boy in surgery initially found himself out of his body, and able to see his parents out in different rooms. But then he was ushered further beyond into Heaven itself, where he had some amazing experiences. Of course, regarding what I've seen, all this is merely conjecture, but there are interesting parallels to what others have mentioned.

The first time I went through the door, I described the cliff edge as not a physical cliff as one might understand it, but rather a demarcation of some kind. In that experience, the area immediately on the other side of the door did not seem dark. However, the perception of lightness and darkness can be relative. On a bright, sunny day, with light coming in through the windows, one might not describe the inside of their house as being dark. However, after spending some time outside in the brilliant sunlight, when returning inside, the house might seem dark in comparison. Now that I've been beyond the cliff edge several times (i.e. the demarcation line), the area immediately beyond the door might seem dark in comparison to the glory of the area beyond.

Likewise, one would normally describe the sun as an extraordinarily intense, incredibly bright object. However, if the entire sun could be compared side-by-side with the infinite glory of God, our blazing sun would actually look like a pitch-black hole in comparison!

It was also fascinating when I was returned to the "lower realm," just beyond the door; I was illuminating that area. I am reminded of where Jesus said, "You are the light of the world." We are to be a spiritual light to those around us. Seeing this demonstrated in such a literal fashion was quite impactful. I'm still meditating on this.

A Christmas Present from Jesus

December 25th Christmas Evening (a continuation)…

I've been sitting for several minutes now just receiving peace from the Lord. I continue to see a banquet table before me. The Lord is at the head of the table. I'm aware of many people at the table. But my attention is drawn to a large box in front of Jesus.

"It's a present for you," Jesus says.

I didn't have any boxed presents this year, but here is Jesus…with one for me! It's quite large, nearly a 2-foot cube. It is covered with something…though I can't see the wrapping in much detail. However, it seems like it has gold and silver threads running through it.

"Open it," Jesus says with a smile.

I put my hands on it, but don't have to forcibly open it…it opens as if in obedience to my desire and thought.

Inside is light. It looks like a ball of light. "Take it," Jesus says.

I pick up the ball of light. It has no hard surface, but has a fuzzy, bright glow and is about foot and a half in diameter. Suddenly it rushes into me and I [physically] jerk as it comes in.

"Ha!" Jesus says and smiles.

"Ha?" I think to myself, a bit puzzled.

"It is my joy I have released into you. You have been asking for it. It is time to release it."

It seems like something inside is resisting this however.

"You must tell it to go," Jesus says.

I commanded whatever was resisting this joy from Jesus, to go in Jesus' name and never return. Something physically thudded in the room when I did this.

"Ha!" Jesus says again.

"Ha!" I say back, almost in jest.

Now I'm seeing pictures of bubbles coming from below, rising up and popping. More and more. It's almost like popcorn popping. I sense it has to do with the joy of the Lord.

"It's been a long time since I've had a really good laugh, Lord."

"Ah, you will! Just focus on Me. Your problems will seem to disappear when you focus on my goodness."

I'm suddenly aware of laughter around me. I can see the table again, with Jesus sitting at the head. Everyone around the table is laughing, including Jesus. That scene lingers on, as the vision seems to be ending...

Part Two: The Adventure Continues

The previously recorded encounters encompassed an eight-month period starting in April 2013. Encouraged by friends to publish them, I wasn't sure when I might cut things off and compile an initial collection. After praying and thinking about it, the first of the new year seemed an appropriate time. So, at the very end of 2013, I compiled what I already experienced. It was a start. Many dozens of the original booklet were printed in my home office and assembled by hand. I was encouraged as they continued to be well received, I added some more as the adventures continued.

The encounters that follow started in January 2014 and continued up to the time this book was initially compiled in 2016.

The last few years have been a time of upheaval. After working and living in the UK for nearly ten years, events surrounding my work led me to returning to Florida. Employment has been uncertain. Living accommodations have been uncertain. Including my relocation from the UK, events forced me to move four times in 17 months! When it came to my vehicles, I've had an engine blow up and a transmission die. Add to this all manner of unplanned for expenses totaling in the thousands of dollars.

However, through all of this the Lord has provided and remained close to my side. Previous encounters already laid a groundwork encouraging me to resolutely trust the Lord — and not fear. However, some of the experiences that follow spoke even more powerfully to this. As a result, when I entered the present time of uncertainty and upheaval, none of it took me by surprise. Through these visions, I had been both forewarned and encouraged to hang on. I am just grateful I was both seeking…and listening. Although I may at times be clueless as to what's happening around me, the Lord knows what He is doing!

As before, these writings contain some fairly personal comments regarding my struggles. Although some of the struggles have not been explicitly identified; the principles — how the Lord deals with them — and especially how He deals with me are what's important. His love, care, guidance and protection are always present for encouragement. And these can be easily discerned, if we are truly willing to pursue Him...and listen.

Trusting in Jesus Casts Out All Fear

I'm standing with my hands in Jesus's hands. He's smiling. We're in a strange place. The ground we are standing on is semi-transparent in many places. There's a lot of red light emanating from below, shining up through the ground. Now it's not just red, but red and yellow. And now it's as if it's being transformed, or revealed and becoming more like fire. It's like we are standing over a huge area of fire...but we are standing well up in the air over it. I feel no heat however.

I have no sense of danger whatsoever. Rather of wonderment. Jesus is still looking at me, smiling. I'm now aware I have my white robe on. The raging fire below causes our robes to blow about a bit.

"What is this place Lord?"

He smiles and laughs a bit. "This is of your own making too." [See note in reflections below.]

"My own making? Do you mean I'm making all this up?"

"No, it's real, but it can't hurt you. I am refining you. You must relax and trust in me."

"You must continue to trust me," Jesus repeats.

"I do trust you Lord; I just place this [experience] in your hands," I say bewildered.

I still see fire all around. It's as if it's burning up something...it's almost raging, but I feel no heat and it's not hurting me.

"Now I want you to do something," Jesus says.

"Ok Lord, what is it?"

"I want you to lean over and look down into the fire." I bend over and do so.

"What do see?" He asks.

"I see a lot of raging fire, Lord."

"But is it hurting you?" He asks.

"No Lord."

I continue to look down into the fire. I see what vaguely looks like a large face down in the fire.

"OK, Lord what is *that*?" I ask apprehensively. "What's happening here?"

He replies, "This is the place of your fears."

"My fears?" I ask incredulously.

"Yes. They look frightening, but are they actually hurting you?" Jesus asks.

"No, they are not." I respond. I suddenly realize and sense, it's because I'm holding Jesus hands.

"Lord, what was that…that looked like a face down in the fire?"

"That was your imagination…it was yet another fear."

This is all very perplexing. "Ok Lord, what next? What are you showing me here?"

He's still holding my hands smiling at me. This is all a very strange experience to be sure.

"I delayed bringing you here, because I knew it would test you. But you *are* trusting me…"

"Oh yes, Lord, I trust you!" I draw close to Jesus and cling to Him. The flames now seem to be larger, hemming us in all around. They look fearsome and make noise, but I am still completely unhurt…and feel absolutely no heat.

I continue to embrace Jesus in the inferno. I am reminded of the three Hebrews who were thrown into the fire, but were completely unhurt, as one "who looked like a son of God" was with them in the flames. I can now even hear crackling around us.

"So, what do you have to fear?" Jesus asks smiling.

"Wow, with You here, absolutely nothing," I reply.

Jesus seems content to just let the inferno keep roaring around us...and just keeps smiling.

"Ok Lord. Is there any reason we need to stay here?"

"No there's not," He replies. "I've been waiting for you to ask."

"So now what?" I enquire.

Jesus replies, "Just say, 'Be gone.'"

I look out and say, "Be gone!"

Suddenly, the fire is gone. We're still standing out in the open air over what appears to be a huge open pit. There's charring from the fire everywhere. Carbon black, or charcoal seems everywhere around.

"So, did the fire hurt you?" Jesus asks.

"No Lord." But I notice that everything around was burnt.

"Fear can indeed destroy, but not when you are with Me—there is no more fear."

"But what happened Lord, when I said, 'Be gone?'"

He replied "You made a choice. You chose to trust me in the midst of the confusion. Trusting me banishes all fear."

"But what about all this blackness, Lord; the stuff that's all burnt?"

"Fear can destroy all that's around you. People fear. Nations fear. It is all subject to destruction. But you cannot be destroyed when you trust in Me. I will always protect you. Even when it appears to be a raging inferno around you, I will never let you go. You can always trust Me."

I seem to be left with the image of me standing with Jesus, up in air over the burnt pit and burned surroundings. But I'm there, completely safe with Jesus.

"Can we leave this place, Lord?"

"Of course. But I don't want you to forget this."

I'm now back just sitting in my chair, but the memory is fresh and will certainly be pondered...

Reflections later:
Earlier this evening, I was rereading experiences from the previous year. Invariably when doing so, I receive fresh insights about those experiences. It was now getting late; just past my bedtime. However, I kept getting glimpses of something. Because of the hour, I was tempted to ignore it. But after rereading my experiences from last year, I was reminded of the need to pursue these visions when they start to occur. I don't know how many times I seemingly forfeited an encounter simply because I didn't pursue it promptly enough.

But I'm also becoming aware of something else. Speaking for myself, I usually have my best experiences with the Lord in the evenings. Recently however, I've typically not been meeting with Him until maybe an hour, or at most two before retiring. I'm now realizing this is not early enough. He wants to spend quality time with me, not just what's left over at the very end of the day. One reason I've missed out on several encounters is the images started so late, I was hesitant to pursue them. If I'm shorted on sleep, I can be in pretty bad shape the next day. I'm realizing this comes down to a re-management of my time. In other words, I need to be seeking Him earlier.

So, it was late—but I decided to pursue it. I really wasn't even convinced anything was going to happen. Initially this experience was a really strange one. It did not unfold very quickly and I was wondering if the Lord really wanted to say something, or not.

As the whole thing slowly unfolded, I was quite perplexed. The environment was very strange and the Lord didn't seem to be volunteering any information. He seemed content to simply stand there holding my hands. It seemed as if I needed to pursue Him...ask questions, because the whole thing had me thoroughly mystified. At the beginning, I was wondering if I wasn't just imagining all of it. However, as the Lord began to instruct me, I began to recognize a certain familiarity in my spirit and settled down.

The phrase, "This is of your own making too," refers back to an encounter I had last year: "A Frank Talk with Jesus — In an Unexpected Place." I met Jesus in a very dark, windswept place. When I enquired what the place was, Jesus responded, *"It is a place of your own making. It is not where I want you to be. I have come to deliver you from this place. We must dismantle the lies and treachery of the enemy. I will heal and deliver you."*

Through the deception of the enemy, we can believe lies and embrace misconceptions that effectively imprison us in a dark place. Last year, the Lord dealt with several such matters from my childhood I had completely forgotten about. Although I've experienced considerable healing through the years, the Lord is never satisfied until a vessel is completely cleaned out.

I think in recent times He's reaching for the "bottom of the barrel" so to speak. That's often where the oldest, yuckiest stuff resides. I don't know if we'll ever be 100% clean in this life, but a barrel that's 98% clean is still far more useful than one that's filled to the brim with toxic waste.

Furthermore, through deception, the enemy can sow fear into us. But that can only happen if we believe the deception. The enemy can infiltrate our thoughts with questions like:

"Does the Lord *really* love me?"

"Will the Lord *really* provide for me?"

"Will the Lord *really* protect me?"

This vision dealt with this head-on. The power of fear was destroying everything around me in a blazing fire. However, I was *completely* safe in the hands of Jesus. I couldn't even feel the heat. Three times Jesus specifically asked if the fire was hurting me, and I responded no. Three additional times I noted myself the fire was not hurting me. The fact that the "fire of fear" couldn't hurt me was repeatedly emphasized. And it was all because I was trusting in Jesus, just holding His hands.

Furthermore, it wasn't even difficult. While holding His hands, it was all very easy. When He told me to speak to the fire, "Be gone!" so it was. Although destruction was evident around me, I was completely unharmed.

One final observation:
Jesus seemed to indicate the destruction I saw around me pertained to other people, even whole nations around me. However, when at the Lord's command I spoke, "Be gone!" the fire that was consuming my surroundings went out. That would suggest that we, as God's people, have the ability to speak peace into the most fearful of circumstances around us. We are to be dispensers of the peace and power of God!

A Visit to A Fiery Place

I see Jesus standing over what appears to be a lake of fire. There are a few big black pillars of rock poking up out of the fire below and around the periphery. It's reminiscent of a volcanic crater filled with magma. I see some steam and smoke coming up from below. The sight beneath me is suggestive of magma, but there are bubbles popping up through it. There are sounds of steam and deep, popping bubbles. Large tongues of fire occasionally rise up around the periphery of what I can see. I wouldn't describe this as a raging fire, but more like a giant, simmering, volcanic cauldron.

I'm standing in an area reminiscent of the other side of the door I've gone through before. Before me is a pathway, but it's not a pathway…it's a stairway. The stairs are of clear material like glass or crystal. They are not joined together like a conventional staircase, but each step floats by itself. They are perhaps about 6 inches thick, maybe three feet wide and about a foot from front to back. The steps ascend into the air and proceed out over the fiery area below. They lead up to a clear, crystal-like platform where Jesus is standing, a couple hundred feet ahead. The crystal platform has railings around it that also appear to be made of clear crystal.

I decide to go up the stairs, but almost instantly I'm up on the platform with Jesus. He's smiling and beckons me forward. We take hands and He just smiles and looks at me.

"Welcome," He says.

I continue to look around us. I can sense only just a little heat from the surroundings. It's just enough so I know it's there, but it is by no means uncomfortable. In my previous vision, I was with Jesus over a fire, but this is completely different. This is an entirely different place.

I continue to stand, holding Jesus' hand and looking about. I can hear some deep bubbling and occasionally hear steam. I just continue to hold His hands, content to just be with Him. I have no fear whatsoever. Jesus starts swinging my arms as He's done before. This is a pretty strange picture, isn't it?

I just want to wait and see what He has for me. He lets out a laugh while still smiling at me. He continues to hold my hands, swinging my arms.

"Well, OK Lord; hear I am."

Interesting... I've now got a view from some distance away. *I can see myself* with Jesus up on the platform. My point of view is revolving around the platform.

Now I can see the same view from overhead, looking down. I've never experienced anything quite like this before, where I can see myself. Now this has my curiosity up. I'm not used to seeing myself and wonder if I can get closer. I now see myself from perhaps ten feet away, standing there in front of Jesus holding His hands. I'm smiling too. My view is now moving to a spot behind myself, looking through to Jesus. I'd like to "go back into myself", but for the moment my point of observation remains behind and somewhat overhead. It's obvious the Spirit is doing something here, but I don't know what. I'm just kind of enjoying it.

"Hey Jesus," I call down to Him. He looks up towards me smiling.

"You see; you can be in two places at once!" He calls out.

Suddenly I'm "back into" myself, then back out again. It's as if I have the ability to be in either position. And then I'm back in.

"OK, Lord," I smile, "What's going on here?"

"Ha, ha," Jesus laughs, "You've just discovered something new in the Spirit."

"OK, Lord, it's pretty interesting, but is there a point?"

"Of course there is," he laughs. "You'll need to contemplate it. It will become apparent to you, in time."

"Ok, Lord; what is this place?" I finally ask.

"It is a holding place," He replies.

"A holding place?"

"It is not *the* lake of fire you were [just] thinking of. That is coming later. But this place is for all sorts of rubbish to be stored until the very end."

I enquire, "Is this related to that 'place of refuse' you once showed me—all the junk that was removed from me? The angels told me all that stuff would be thrown in the lake of fire at the end."

Jesus replies, "No, this is a different place for a different purpose."

From the vantage point over myself, I see what looks like a form, a spirit being pulled out of me. Jesus waves His hand and it vanishes. "This is the abyss," He says. "All sorts of foul things are imprisoned here waiting for the final judgment."

"I'm not sure why you're showing me this, Lord."

"That too will become apparent in time." Jesus replies.

I continue to stand with Jesus on the platform. "Can I look about a bit?" I ask.

"Of course," Jesus says.

I walk over to the railing. As I get to it, I can now feel a huge heat not only from below, but seemingly all around. I step back from the railing and it nearly vanishes. I'm not sure why I'm being shown all this, but I'm safe and in no rush to depart. I guess I'm just trying to take it in.

"OK, that's enough for now," Jesus says. "Unless you want something," He adds.

"Yes, Lord. If you got rid of a spirit that was pestering me, how about getting rid of more? How about all of it?" Jesus laughs. "Of course, all you had to do was ask. This is a place of purging." Jesus extends His hand towards me. I can hear what sounds like a bunch of upset voices. A whole bunch of things are cast away and vanish.

"There will be more," Jesus says. "We are cleaning you out. But we must do so in an orderly fashion that brings the greatest glory to the Father."

"OK Lord, whatever you say."

"And if you find something yourself you don't like, command it to leave you and I will send it here. Anything that is sent here can no longer get out and harass you anymore."

I'm now standing again at the base of the stairs seeing Jesus above. But then Jesus suddenly appears in front of me.

"You will come back here, for there is more to show you. But that is enough for now. I bless you with My peace. My peace I impart to you. Go now and contemplate what you have seen."

I now find myself outside the door I've gone through before. I push down the handle and open it again. Jesus is still standing there smiling at me. I know I can come back through whenever I need to…or when He calls.

"OK, good night Lord," I say and close the door.

"Good night," He says.

Reflections afterwards…

This is easily the strangest experience I've had so far. I think I have a lot more questions than answers. Perhaps the biggest is, why would Jesus show me something like this? I've never had any interest in places like this. What's the point? Obviously, there is one, I'll just have to wait, ponder and eventually discover what it is.

During the entire experience, I never had any unpleasant feelings at all. Instead I just sort of took it all in, as best I could. Jesus just seemed to be happy I was there with Him.

I would say I saw all of it at a level of clarity that's a notch above my previous experiences...in particular, the clear steps; the pathway up to Jesus. And then there were those points of observation "outside myself" where I could see myself standing in front of Jesus. That's still a bit of a mystery, though it does have Biblical precedent. In the book of Daniel, we read:

"In the third year of King Belshazzar's reign, I, Daniel, had a vision... In my vision *I saw myself* in the citadel of Susa..."
— Daniel 8:1,2

So, for at least part of his vision, Daniel was watching from a point outside himself...and he could see himself in the vision.

Afterwards, I wondered if anyone else had seen a place like this, so I did a quick Google search. I came across an online article entitled, "A Survey of the Abyss in the Old and New Testaments." In it, the author collected all Old and New Testament scriptures mentioning, or seemingly related to the abyss. I found Revelation 9:2 particularly interesting: *"When he opened the Abyss, smoke rose from it like the smoke from a gigantic furnace."* That imagery would certainly line up with my experience.

There are also scriptures mentioning an angel having "the key" to the abyss — that it is a place where evil spirits and satan himself will be imprisoned. The fact it is a place of imprisonment also confirms what I was told in my experience. Interestingly, I've paid little attention to these scriptures in the past — I've never had any interest in such things. (And I still don't. I'd much rather focus on Jesus.) However, He's shown me this for a reason...

When Jesus was casting what appeared to be evil spirits away from me, He said, "This is a place of purging." I sensed He was not referring to the abyss itself, but rather to my experience there with Him. And I'm not certain whether or not something actually happened to me at that moment, or whether it was a picture of an ongoing process. Jesus definitely indicated there would be more to come. I think the passage of time will reveal further answers to these questions.

There is no question impure spirits can be assigned by the enemy to cause us grief. Paul identified his thorn in the flesh to be a "messenger of satan." Sometimes, for reasons known only to the Lord, we may be allowed to be buffeted by these things for a season. For example, during the last year I have been under significant financial duress. So many, many things went wrong, I wondered on several occasions if the enemy wasn't messing with me behind the scenes. However, the Lord made use of those difficult times to produce positive spiritual benefits. Had I not been under the financial restrictions experienced last year, I wouldn't have been in a position to receive those spiritual blessings. So yes, in our lives there's more refining to be done, but Jesus knows the right order and time to address these issues.

From a "technical standpoint," I found the following statement interesting: *"And if you find something yourself you don't like, command it to leave you and I will send it here. Anything that is sent here can no longer get out and harass you anymore."* There was a time in deliverance ministries a few years back, where people were commanding demons to "go into the abyss." In recent years, most have backed away from that approach because the scriptures don't actually teach we have the authority to do that. Rather, the approach today is to command the demon to leave and "go to Jesus" or, "go where Jesus sends you." My experience here would seem to confirm that is the most appropriate approach. Jesus said, *"…command it to leave you and I will send it here."* We command it to go in Jesus name, but after that it is in His domain…where He will deal with it as He wishes.

And then at the end, Jesus said He will bring me back there some day to show me something else. In one sense, I really have no desire to go back there. However, if Jesus wants me too, then by all means I will do so. In the meantime, I still have a lot of questions about why He would show this to me in the first place… I think I will share this with some friends as well and see if anyone can shed further thoughts on these matters…

Increasing Beauty

Last night I was spending time with the Lord and began to see a familiar place. It was the place "of my own making" that Jesus was cleaning up. The first visit was almost in total darkness, except for Jesus, Himself. In the second, I began to see more things as Jesus was cleaning…

I was back standing in a flat place, apparently up along a high hill or mountainside. Before it was a cleared area with lots of rocks around the edges. Now however, it was quite different.

The area I was standing in was nicely clean like a parking area, with a road out ahead that seemed to go down the hillside. The "parking area" (maybe 150' across) and road were covered with small, angular, cream or sand colored rocks. The area looked freshly covered and raked out nicely. There appeared to be something like a curb around this area, nicely separating the stones from a berm of ground just outside the curb. Grass covered the ground over the berm and there were lots of small bushes, maybe 2 feet high planted all along the top of the berm. It's as if someone has been busy landscaping the area.

There was a bright, blue sky with brilliant sunshine. As I recount this, I'm starting to see this all again… I see beautiful, high green hills in the distance. Like my previous visits, there's a valley below with a small river meandering through it. Suddenly the Lord is by my side in the "parking area".

"Come, let's have look around," He says.

"Wow things have been changing here," I say. "It's a lot more beautiful than before."

Jesus smiles, "It's progressing."

At one point I found myself down at the river, in the midst of a green, grassy flood plain (or so it appeared). As a result of some previous visions, I immediately thought of the water. In past visions, it's often represented the Spirit. However, in this place, I sense it is representing my spirit.

I placed my foot into the water (and now do so again). The experience is strange. There appears to be hot and cold currents within the waters. One moment, a hot current of water hits my foot, suddenly displaced and followed by a cold one. I can feel these hot and cold currents flowing around my foot.

Jesus is there, just a few feet away in the grass and smiling.

"What does this mean Lord?" I ask.

Jesus smiles and laughs, "I think you already know the answer."

He's right of course. I've already sensed it... If this is the river of my own spirit, there are things both hot and cold flowing within it. I think the hot represents something positive. Perhaps the passions I have for Jesus and His kingdom. The cold represents things not yet yielded and conformed to His desires. There are areas within my life that have yet to be kindled with His passion. I'll have to give this more thought. Oh, that the river of my spirit would be boiling for Him!

I'm now standing at a distance, partway back up the hill and overlooking the river...and I now see the river as boiling! I'll claim that as something prophetic!

My attention is also drawn to other surroundings. In my previous visions here, I saw numerous black rocks lying about. I was told these represented impurities in my life the Lord was cleaning up. I still see a few here and there, but not as many, most are pretty small; a few inches across. Interestingly, there were no black rocks at all at my entry point (the parking area). That area was nicely cleaned up and landscaped.

What all these represent, I'm not yet certain. The place is far more beautiful than I last saw it. And I suspect I'll be coming back...

Reflections afterwards...
About two weeks after this experience we were singing a song in church, "I Could Sing of Your Love Forever." The verse goes as follows:
"Over the mountains and the seas, your river runs with love for me And I will open my heart and let the healer set me free."

While singing, I saw the scene again, standing by the river. I could also see a number of small yellow flowers growing up amongst the grass along the stream's edge. (I actually saw glimpses of this several times since the original vision.)

However, as we were singing the above words, something came to me regarding the hot and cold currents running in the stream. More specifically, the hot currents originated from the Lord Himself. They were of Him. These were working their way through the cold water of my own spirit. I suspect the intent is to warm all the water of my spirit; the hot displacing the cold. Interesting...

Another Missed Opportunity

I've been seeing the door I've gone through before. I wasn't writing yesterday, but pushed down the handle, opened it up and went through. There was a very bright spot of light in the distance. It was very intense and seemed to be showing in my direction. Again, the area immediately around the door was somewhat dark, but the powerful, almost beam of light shining in my direction illumined almost the whole area. The only darker areas were up against what appeared to be a sort of barrier...that the door goes through.

I looked forward into the light, which almost seemed to be coming through a tunnel. I tried to go forward, but didn't get very far. I suspect I'm supposed to be writing these things down as they happen, so I'm back tonight ready to do so.

I can see the door in front of me. I push down the handle and open it. Again, I see the bright light in the distance, although it seems farther away. The bright beam of light doesn't reach all the way here but stops a way out beyond the cliff edge.

"Well Lord, have I missed it? Have I waited too long?" An angel appears to my left. I'm aware there's another one to my right, but I don't seem permitted to fully see him.

As they hold me, they lift me up. Odd, It's as if I can see myself now. The angels are lifting me up and taking me forward to the tunnel of light.

"You only just made it," one says.

I know I should have pursued this sooner. "Forgive me Lord."

I see the bright light out in front of me. The light is coming closer. Jesus is in the light.

"I've had an experience waiting for you here, but you missed it...for now," Jesus says.

"Oh, Lord, I'm so sorry. Why am I so slow? I need so much more determination. To jump on things right away."

He's looking at me lovingly, but I know He's trying to teach me a lesson too. I need to respond to Him right away.

He seems to be receding further away. The angels have put me back down into the area just before the cliff. The cliff area is very dark in comparison the light in the distance.
I can still see the light in the distance, but sense it's time to leave for the moment. I go back out through the door.

Reflections afterward:
My first mistake was not writing things down when the vision first appeared the previous day. It's become increasingly apparent the Lord wants me to record these as they happen. If I don't...the vision will not proceed.

The second mistake: not pursing the Lord earlier in the evening (again) and then thinking I'll just investigate first thing in the morning. At least that was my intent, but things didn't work out that way.

I had a lot on the agenda for the day and went straight to work. I then planned on pursuing the vision during the afternoon, but a project at work got extended... I then had a commitment this evening I needed to attend. Get the picture?

After opening the door and seeing the beam of light no longer reaching me, I instinctively knew what was happening. I knew I missed it. It was a huge mistake. I should have pursued this right away this morning...if not last night. How can I be so dense? How is it I keep doing this kind of thing? I guess I have to learn to ramp up my determination, no matter what.

Interestingly, I can now again get glimpses of the light coming right up to the door again. So, tomorrow morning, first thing, I will pursue this!

Comment some time later:

I should make it clear, the vision for that evening was indeed over. The further "glimpses" I referred to were a message that more would be coming later. It's hard to describe, but one often understands these things in the spirit. There are times I would get a glimpse, or repeated glimpses of something during the day while working, or perhaps driving, or even while taking a shower — accompanied by an internal witness it's an invitation to purse as soon as possible.

"I Just Want You to Be with Me"

I've opened the door and there's bright light beyond. I see what looks like a tunnel with the bright light ahead in it. Jesus is in the light. His arms beckon to me.

I'm not seeing the tunnel anymore. The light is out in front of me. There are some clouds below and beyond. There are lots of bright colors around among the clouds and what looks like sky.

"Jesus, I want you. I need you. I want to get closer to you."

Now I see Him closer to me, again with arms outstretched. "I love you," He says.

"Lord I just want to see you clearer." He's closer now. I feel His arms and take His hands.
I can't see His face however, ...there's so much light.

"I just want you to be with me," He says. "You must continue to push into Me...toward Me.

I'm a bit disappointed I don't seem to be going anywhere or doing anything...but Jesus is here...that's the important thing.

"Lord, I'm sorry, if I haven't fully appreciated some of the visions I've had so far. Even if you just show up and we don't do anything or go anywhere, I trust You. It's good enough for me. I accept what you are providing."

The vision fades and I'm back outside the door.

Reflections afterwards:
I did not pursue this vision the following morning as I anticipated a few nights ago. For the next three days, it just didn't seem to "be there." You can't manufacture this stuff, so I waited until I started seeing something again.

I just finished reading a book where the author claims to have had many "Third Heaven" visits and says these continue to occur. The book contains a lot of thought provoking material. He says the Lord wants us to visit Him there, but there can be many blockages. Some of these are obvious, such as living in willful sin. Others are subtler, but nonetheless can block the way. Towards the end of the book he gets into the "nitty-gritty" so to speak, where he discusses the question: What cost are we willing to pay? I have been contemplating that very issue lately.

However, I'm also learning (again) the necessity of not belittling even the "smallest things" The Lord gives us. I would love to have some "third heaven" experiences — though not for the experiences themselves. Rather, I would be desirous of such things *only* if they provide an avenue to an even deeper, intimate relationship with the Lord. Ultimately of course, the Lord is the one who chooses how we approach Him. Our job is to continue pursuing…and remain open to what He wishes to do.

But we need to start someplace. Some, for whatever reason (known only to the Lord) seem to launch into such experiences seemingly from day one. Others like myself, need to pursue. And indeed, this seems to be the norm. The author of that book testified he pursued for years.

I have to learn not to become impatient. There is a cost…and part of that involves a further investment of time. I must not despise even the "smallest" of visions. I have therefore determined to appreciate, even relish the smallest of experiences. I might not see clearly. Some experiences might be simple and not last long. But I will appreciate them and thank the Lord for them nonetheless. I am determined to be appreciative and thankful for everything the Lord gives me, even if it is seemingly "small" at the time.

I also have a sense (that's how I might describe it) I might be sharing these insights with others in the future. I feel I need to pay attention to these things and make note of them.

Root Pruning

I continue to experience "mini-visions" where I simply go through the door and meet with Jesus. We don't go anywhere. He just wants to spend time with me. One time, He came through the door to me. Another time, it was as if He and the door were somehow "merged" together as I beheld Him. I was reminded of the scriptures where Jesus said, "I am the door," and "I am the way."

Several years ago, I had an unusual (for me) encounter with the Lord at a Christian conference in Mallorca. I had never experienced anything like it before. One beautiful afternoon, I was sitting out on my hotel balcony quietly worshiping the Lord. Suddenly, something like a great bolt of energy shot through and shook my whole body with considerable force. I was utterly perplexed not knowing what had just happened. Then it happened again…and again. By the fourth time I was on my feet not knowing what to do. I sensed something powerful was happening in my spirit…but what? I was completely bewildered.

Not knowing what might happen next, I thought it best to go back into my room. I knelt by my bed, still in an attitude of prayer as these surges continued to jolt me. As I remained bowed before the Lord, the individual jolts turned into continuous shaking. My arms in particular were shaking incredibly.

This continued for at least an hour and a half…and the evening dinner hour was approaching. I decided I wouldn't attempt to go into the dining room in this state…I doubted my ability to hold any utensils and feed myself! So, I abstained from the meal and chose to remain in this unusual state with the Lord.

Now there is something I must make very clear. This was *not* some kind of hyper-emotional experience. I'm not the kind of person who gets emotionally giddy. In fact, I was emotionally very calm. My mind was very calm. But deep down, something powerful was happening *in my spirit*.

My rational mind was, if anything perplexed. My rational self (which is usually my dominant feature) was watching all this bewildered and asking, "Doug, what on earth is going on with you?? This is nuts..." However, I sensed the Holy Spirit was doing *something*, so I told myself to just allow things to run their course.

After several hours of this, it was time for the evening session of the conference. I managed to gather myself together and went down to the conference room. Not wanting to draw attention to myself, I remained and stood in the back of the room for the entire evening...still shaking continuously.

As I retired for the evening, I was still getting jolts. I told the Lord I appreciated whatever He was doing...but could He kindly have some mercy and allow me to fall asleep? I eventually dozed off.

Since that time, I continue to have periods where I "get the shakes" in the Lord's presence. Recently, this has become a bit more prevalent again. However, I've wondered about this many times. It seems like after these experiences, there's no change in my life, no change in condition, no further victory. I've had occasion to wonder if it's really the Lord doing something, or just some psychological craziness of mine.

Interestingly, it's *never* associated with any kind of emotional excitement. Rather it only occurs when I'm contemplating the things of the Lord and seeking Him. It's as if my spirit within me is reaching out, desperately yearning for more of Him. It's like something is going on under the surface — but I don't know what.

Today, I was talking with the Lord about this again, wondering what it was all about. I suddenly had a vision of a large tree being lifted out of the ground with a large root ball. I could see lots of small roots on the outside of the ball and was somehow aware this tree had been "root pruned" in preparation for being transplanted. With my landscaping hobby, I knew what root pruning was for, but decided to look it up on the internet just to see what else I might learn. The following are excerpts from an article on the subject:

Root pruning is the process of severing the roots of an established tree that is going to be dug and transplanted, to encourage the growth of new feeder roots inside the root ball that will be moved with the tree.

Established trees that have been growing in the ground have roots that reach out far beyond the branches or drip line. These long roots are used by the tree to anchor and support it. However most of the small feeder roots, which bring in food and nutrients to the tree, are likely to be found towards the end of the main roots, some distance from the tree itself.

When a tree is dug for moving and transplanting, generally the ground is dug at the circumference of the drip line, sometimes less. To encourage the development of feeder roots closer to the drip line, root pruning is done.

Root pruning involves severing the roots of a tree, all the way around the tree's circumference at the drip line. This can be done by slicing down with a sharp spade. **Ideally, root pruning should take place a year prior to digging and transplanting the tree.**

For example, nurseries which grow tree seedlings in the ground, will root prune the seedlings the year before they are dug, balled and wrapped.

If a large, mature tree were simply dug up and moved, it would likely be killed. The major disruption to the root system would destroy it. With root pruning, the tree is left in place so as to minimize any disturbance. The pruning causes many new roots to develop close in to the tree. After a year, the tree can be successfully dug out with most of the feeder roots now intact, close to the tree.

The interesting thing to note is this: There is no *observable* difference to the tree when the root pruning is performed. However, under the surface hidden from sight, things are indeed happening. In other words, *it's a time of preparation for a major event that will take place.*

In John 15:1-6, Jesus describes us as vines whom the Father prunes to produce more fruit. That kind of pruning however, is visible. If we are at all spiritually observant, we often recognize when we are being "pruned." In fact, even our family and close friends might also recognize when we are being pruned.

However, after a plant is root pruned, there are typically no *visible* results. The process does indeed result in a type of growth—but it is something not *visibly* discernable at the moment.

I had a sense, that the Lord has been very gentle, yet deliberate with me. He's been pruning roots, but one at a time, getting me ready for something. Many times, especially when the smaller roots are cut, I might not be aware it's even happening. Other times, there might be some discomfort, but it passes.

Like a tree, if the Lord were to simply cut all my roots at once and immediately transplant me (like instantly launching me into some new ministry), I might not be able to handle the shock. Fortunately, He knows the best way to properly prepare us.

As mentioned, the scriptures do paint a picture of the Lord pruning our branches. And that is something visible. However, this insight shows how He may also be pruning our roots. There may be no immediate, *visible* results. But that doesn't mean something significant isn't happening. *Preparation is taking place.*

> **Only after the root system has been pruned *and healed*, can the tree be transplanted into its new location.**

An Unexpected Person Encourages Me:
Trust in Jesus

I'm standing at the old door. I push down on the handle and push the door open. It's very bright on the other side. A figure is standing there with very bright light behind him. I'm not sure if it's Jesus or not. At first, I thought it might be, but he is frequently the source of the light. This time the light is behind the figure. I get the impression this is someone else.

The front of the person is somewhat shaded because of all the light coming from behind. I can make out he's smiling at me. His hair is not very long, but quite curly, which runs down into a full, but not long beard…no more than an inch, or so long. He's wearing a white robe with a leather belt around the middle. I can also see he's wearing leather sandals.

"Hello sir, I'm not certain who you are," I say cautiously.

He laughs, "I'm here to visit you."

I'm still standing outside the door looking in. A little apprehensive, not knowing what to expect I pray, "Well Lord Jesus, I just put this all before you. I trust that you're in this and guiding it somehow."

"Come forward," the man says. I step through the door. We are standing between the door and the cliff's edge.

"This is a test," he says. "We wanted to see if you would come forward."

"Well, I'm uncertain what's going on, but I've put it into the Lord's hands and I trust Him."

The man responds, "There is much coming where you will have to trust Him."

I'm still puzzled by what's happening here. "Can I ask who you are?"

"Of course you can, I've been waiting for you to ask. I'm Peter."

"Peter???" I ask, utterly stunned.

"You remember the story when the Lord asked me to step out of the boat and join Him on the water?"

"Of course, sir."

"I had to trust Him, even though I didn't know what I was doing. My trust waivered briefly, but as always, Jesus was faithful and caught me. Together we walked back to the boat."

"Yes, I remember the story."

"So it will be with you. You will have to trust Him even though you might not understand what is happening around you."

"Am I going to have to go through another storm?" I ask.

"Perhaps, but the storm is not important. Trusting the Lord in all that happens—that's what's important."

He extends his hands out towards me. They are very large and seem rugged.

"I worked with these hands all my life. I supported myself and my family with them. But there came a time when my own hands were not enough. I had to trust the Lord with my life, my family and my friends. This is the level of trust you are being called to."

I take his hands into mine.

"There are many others like you coming along as well," he says.

"Coming along?" I wonder.

"There is a great adventure lying before you, but as in my little adventure in the boat, trusting the Lord is paramount. It is the secret to victory."

There is suddenly a swirl of what looks like water in front of me and around Peter, which engulfs him. For a moment, I continue to hold his hands, but then they are released. The swirling water and Peter disappear. All that remains is the light in the distance. Although I can no longer see Peter, I sense that he is watching me.

The swirl of water has left everything fresh on the edge of the cliff. Intense bright light still emanates towards me from a distance.

I'm standing outside the door again. Oddly, I don't feel a need to close it. It's as if the light is shining right through the door opening out to where I am. It's almost as if the door is not meant to be closed…but stay open…

Reflections afterwards:
If I encounter anyone but the Lord or angels, I immediately become apprehensive. After all, there are other spiritual entities out there that do not have our best interests in mind. Deception is always a possibility, so I maintain my guard. I always go into these visions with the Lord centered in my thoughts. Therefore, when encountering someone unknown like this, I always and immediately give the situation to the Lord. I typically ask Him to end the experience if it is not of Him. However, if it is of Him, allow it to continue. I have no choice but to place my trust fully in Him…trusting that He will watch over and protect me.

Of course, if we let fear of the unknown overtake us, we might never experience anything. So though being guarded in such situations, I'm prepared to move forwards…but overtly place my trust totally in the Lord and trust He is in complete control.

The Lord has spoken to me before about trusting Him, but this encounter was perhaps the most riveting yet.

Often after these experiences I step back out from the door and close it. However, this time the end of the experience was distinctly different. I was back outside, but the door remained open. Light was shining from the heavenly realm through the door out to where I was…and there was a distinct impression the door was to remain open.

I've been reading several books about "third heaven" experiences as I continue to push into getting closer to the Lord; experiences where tastes of heaven come to earth. I sense the door remaining open is an encouragement from the Lord and a sign He wants nothing in the way between Him and His people. It may represent what some call, "an open heaven." I will continue to meditate on this.

However, even now as I look into the spirit, I can still see the door wide open with the light of heaven shining through…

Impeding the Flow of the Spirit

I've been seeing the place with the stream running through the valley. I'm standing near the stream's edge. This was the stream that represented my own spirit. The last time I was here, there were small yellow flowers along the stream's edge, in amongst the beautiful, soft green grass. Now, I also see small purple flowers growing up amongst them.

As I step close to the edge of the stream, my left shoe suddenly gets a little water in it. There are marshy spots along the edge.

As before, it's a beautiful sunny day, with blue skies. I'm aware of the Lord's presence close by, though I can't see Him clearly. Instead my attention is drawn to a small rock in the center of the stream. It's perhaps four or five inches across. As the water hits it, the flow is disturbed since the water must flow around it. My attention seems focused on this, so I know there's some significance here.

I ask the Lord what this rock is.

"Stubbornness," is the reply.

"OK, Lord, I guess that's pretty self-explanatory. So, I assume there are some areas of my life that I've been reluctant to change…or perhaps attitudes?" "Some of both," He replies.

I reach for the rock and lift it up. There was some black muck holding it in place. After the muck is washed off, I release it and the current carries the rock away…it disappears and no longer can be seen. I note the stream now flows freely over the place the rock used to be.

I can see the Lord more clearly now, standing a short distance away, smiling at me. I could ask Him what this all means, but I already sense what's going on.

The rock was stuck in place. It really wasn't at all difficult to pull up, but did require a deliberate act of my will to do so. I am aware the Holy Spirit is mingled in with the flow of my own spirit. The rock however, stopped the flow altogether and forced the water to flow around it. In my own experience working with water, I know this kind of interruption of flow decreases efficiency and performance…energy is lost in the process.

"OK, Lord, I think I see the point. Such things are like mini-blockages that need to be removed in order for the things of the spirit to flow unimpeded. But I must be willing to take action when such things are revealed."

"So Lord, I just submit myself to You. I ask Holy Spirit that You reveal whatever blockages like this need to be removed. May I see them clearly and have the determination to act…and repent regarding whatever You show me. In Jesus' name, Amen."

Joining Together with Jesus

The last couple days I continue to see the stream running through the field. I've often looked up towards the source to see if I could discern it, but was never able to. It seems like the Holy Spirit guides these things. I do make an effort to look around, so I don't miss anything. However, it often seems my attention is guided and focused on whatever the Lord has to show me for the moment. Such was the case when I previously focused on the stone in the stream.

However, now I have been able to look and walk further upstream. I came to a large pool, perhaps twenty-five feet across. To my surprise, it was red. However, it was not the source. Perhaps another fifty feet or so further upstream was a smaller pool, maybe four feet across. The stream seems to originate here. The water was clear and cold. It flows out into a stream a few feet across and gets a bit wider as it enters the larger, red pool. The water in the red pool seems very warm. Water continues on its journey out of the red pool into a much larger stream, maybe five or six feet across. Wisps of red flow out of the large pool into the stream where all the water is again clear.

I sense this is the origin of the hot and cold currents I've detected in the stream. The cold water originates in the small spring at the headwater. This in turn flows into the red pool, which is very warm. The red wisps flow out into the stream as it continues, but they visibly disappear after about 10-15 feet. Though the water is visibly clear from that point on, there are still separate hot and cold currents in the stream.

As I look about, I notice the grass does not seem as fresh in this area. There's some brown blades mixed in here and there. Also, the yellow and purple flowers I saw downstream are not here. There are flowers here, but they are quite different. They are white, very small, only a quarter inch across. They're kind of like little, finely-petaled globes on top of thin stems that are maybe about a foot high. Despite this being the apparent headwaters, the area seems dryer. I now also see what looks like older, dryer plants giving off seeds floating away in the air.

What I saw further downstream was beautiful, fresh vibrant green grass. I would describe that area as being more spring-like. However, this area has more of an end-of-summer, or early fall look to it.

Reflections afterwards:
I've been thinking about this for several days. My past experiences have shown that much of what I've seen in this place are symbolic. For example, black rocks represent impurities in my life. The stream itself is the flow of my own spirit, which contains both hot and cold currents.

Again, I struggle with symbolism, as it's not my preferred language. I'm more comfortable with the language of my rational mind. However, I know the Lord wants me to ponder these things and so I shall.

I quickly perceived the large, warm, red pool as having an association with Jesus and His blood. However, the small pool has required a bit more pondering.

The small pool with cold, clear water was the headwater of my own spirit. Normally, from our earthly perspective, we consider cold, clear water to be desirable. However, in this case I sensed the Holy Spirit was showing me something different. In reality, water in such a spring is not only cold, but also sterile. There is no life in it. There is something missing: the Lord.

The headwater also originated in an area that was not very lush. Things were dry and tired looking with seeds floating about, like late summer. This was a bit surprising and took even more pondering.

I realize that I am the "seed" of my parents. I was also born into imperfection. Unlike the Garden of Eden, I was born into a scene of semi-dryness. This was not God's original plan. My young spirit—though one might initially think as being pure—was in fact, actually lacking, separated from God by sin and imperfection. This remained the case until my spirit encountered Jesus through the Holy Spirit. Our spirits mingled together forming a new stream...

Jesus Our Protector

I see a fir tree. It's in the shape of a traditional Christmas tree. The wind is blowing through the branches. I hear birds cheeping and see some in among the branches. The birds are fluttering in and out of the branches. The wind is now picking up and really starting to throw the tree about. The birds are no longer cheeping and are hunkered down inside the tree, clinging to the branches. I can hear the wind whistling about.

I now see the Lord standing immediately behind the tree, opening up His arms. He continues to stand behind the tree, almost touching it.

I now also see some kind of large creature out to the left and front of the tree. It's big and brutish. It stands on its legs like a man, but seems more like a big ape. However, it has what appears like clothing on, but consisting of many tattered strips. It appears to be the source of the wind as it blows out of its mouth, powerfully towards the tree. I can sense it's trying to blow even harder, as it tenses its muscles and blows with even greater effort, showing off its seemingly great strength.

Interestingly however, it's standing perhaps 10-12 feet away and doesn't seem to want to step closer. Not with Jesus standing behind the tree.

Every so often Jesus places His arms closer and part way around the tree. As the beast tries to blow more forcefully, Jesus is right behind the tree and places His arms part way around...almost as if He is supporting and shielding it from the worst of the blasts.

The creature finally wears out, drops its arms seemingly downtrodden. The birds now start fluttering around again, some coming out and sit on Jesus' clothes; a few even sit on His head.

Reflections afterwards...
This certainly appears to be speaking about the Lord's protection. The tree itself is a form a provision. It's a place for the birds to rest...or in this case, take refuge. However, the tree has its limits. It can only provide so much cover. When things start getting really bad, the Lord steps in and provides additional protection with His presence. And you could see it was totally effortless for Him.

I could sense the beast did not want to get closer. Rather it stood at a distance, but put on a good show. The clothing, if you could call it that, was a bunch of tattered strips perhaps about 4 inches long. It was reminiscent of a mummy's wrappings, but torn to bits. There was nothing on the head, but was quite hairy. As the beast blew, I could see it tensing its muscles, as if to show how strong and powerful it was. However, I could also sense this was largely for show. In reality, it didn't have all that much power, *especially* in the presence of Jesus!

The beast was finally forced to give up, resigned to defeat. The area in which it stood became shadowed and faded from view, with my attention fully again on Jesus, the tree and the birds.

Interestingly, Jesus did allow the tree to be buffeted about, with the birds clinging inside. However, he never let the force become so great, the tree and birds inside were in any real danger. Yes, the birds were buffeted about by the enemy, but the Lord used the experience to demonstrate His unquestioned superiority and protection.

"While I was with them, I protected them and kept them safe by that name you gave me." *John 17:12*

"In the same way your Father in heaven is not willing that any of these little ones should perish." *Matthew 18:14*

Preparation for A Feast

I see the open door before me; there's much light on the other side shining out. I push the door completely open and walk through. I'm wearing my white robe and have a gold band on my head.

The light is very intense beyond the cliff edge. I can't see a path this time. Only a wall of light. I have no fear and simply step into the light. It's almost like I stepped through a nice warm, fuzzy barrier of air into the light beyond. There's light everywhere. I now can make out a path ahead. Interestingly it's not gold, but like an off-white, almost shiny cobblestone. I step out onto it and find it to be a bit slippery. Very strange. But I've seen strange things before and choose to trust the Lord.

"Lord, I'm not sure what's happening here, but I place my trust totally in You."
I find I don't have to walk on the path. All I have to do is think about going forward and I start sliding forward with my feet flat on the surface. It's reminiscent of skiing, except this is much easier.

I've now gone through what was like a milky white, cloudy area out into open sky with the path proceeding out ahead of me. I continue to slide forward along the path and suddenly hear, "Stop." I do so. There's a lot of light up to my upper left, which is where I've seen a golden city in the past. What I see however, is a spherical, white cloud, but it's not a cloud. It appears to be myriads of angels swirling about all over the place—a huge cloud of them. The path does not head towards them, but rather continues out into the distance.

My attention however is on the cloud of angels. An angel appears to my left and lifts me off the path. I'm slowly taken toward to the cloud of angels. There is a myriad of sounds. I hear what sounds like thousands of instruments and voices all mixed together. However, there's no single melody. It reminds me of an orchestra warming up.

The angel asks, "Would you like to join them?"

"Yes, certainly," I reply.

I'm up at the edge of the cloud of angels.

"They are composing," the angel next to me says.

"Composing?" I ask.

"Yes, they are composing music for a great feast that is about to take place. The Master wants everything to be perfect, and so shall it be."

"What is the feast for?" I enquire.

"It's for you," was the reply.

"For me?!" I am shocked. I assumed it might be a feast for the entire bride of Christ… or something like that.

"That will come later," the angel says. "This feast is just for you." I'm stunned.

"The Father has so many resources available, this is easy to do. He has much He wants to lavish on you."

I'm completely overwhelmed.

"There are special delicacies He's prepared just for you. These will help sustain you for what lies ahead."

"And what about this music?" I ask.

"Earlier you requested to hear the music of the angels. You had in mind music for worshiping God. That continues here — continually. However, this is being composed just for you. The Father wants to sing a love song to you and nothing is too good for that. We will sing with Him."

I'm utterly speechless.

"When will this happen?" I finally ask.

"Shortly. The preparations are still being made. It will happen when you least expect it. The Father loves to surprise His people."

The cloud is so bright with the angelic light everywhere and I still hear a myriad of sounds. The angel next to me smiles.

"Wow what's next," I ask.

"That's up to you," he replies.

"Wow, I have to confess I need to process this and think about it."

"Of course. Remember you can always come back through the door when you need to. It's always open to you."

I suddenly find myself sliding backwards along the path, back through the warm, lit area. I pause briefly wondering what this area is. But then I slide back to the cliff edge and back up next to the door. I back up out of the door, while still facing it. It remains open, with the light in the distance.

Reflections afterwards:
The Lord would throw a huge feast for me? Just for me? He would sing accompanied by a magnificent myriad of angelic hosts? Just for me??? It doesn't seem possible, but I know it's true. But I'm still left utterly stunned.

The path at first, seemed a bit strange. But I've been learning when it comes to things of the spiritual realm: expect the unexpected! Again, I would have expected to see a path of gold, however, as I think about it, I've seen other kinds of paths too. The fact is, God is infinitely creative and not limited by our preconceived notions. I am reminded of Ephesians 3:20, "Now to Him who is able to do immeasurably more than all we ask or imagine..." There is so much in the heavenly realms we can't even *begin* to imagine.

Earlier in the evening I had been talking with the Lord, desiring to hear the angels singing praises to Him. The angel when referring to this made a statement I found quite interesting.

"Earlier you requested to hear the music of the angels. You had in mind music for worshiping God. That continues here — continually." Later when looking back at this, I thought the phrase, "That continues here — continually," was a bit unusual.

Normally one wouldn't use what is essentially the same word twice in sentence. However, it's what he said. While pondering this, I remembered reading something. Scholars have noted that Biblical writers sometimes used "double positives" or "double negatives" within a given phrase for the purpose of special emphasis. In this case, "That (i.e., praise) continues here — continually," would suggest an emphasis on the *nonstop*, perpetual praising of God in heaven. I found this interesting. It's as if human language cannot truly describe the eternal nature what's happening there.

On a completely different matter... Traveling on the path was quite interesting. Just by thinking, I started to slide forward. I've noticed this kind of thing before. Just by thinking about your destination, you can go there almost instantly. However, sliding like this along the path was something different from anything I previously experienced.

As I was reviewing this experience in my mind, I suddenly had a startling realization. My legs were straight!! This both surprised and amazed me. Allow me to explain...

I was born with congenital defects in both my legs. There are issues with both my hips, upper and lower leg bones. My knees tend to point in while my feet point out. What this means is, it's physically impossible for me to stand with both feet pointed forward, legs parallel and slightly bent, as one would ski. However, in this vision that's what I was doing! My legs were both parallel and pointing forward. It's the first time in my life I've actually experienced that. So, though my physical body may have defects, the spiritual one does not!

While contemplating this, I'm amazed how things seemingly unrelated to the message of a vision can surface and have an impact all their own...

The Impact of the Cross

I was attending a conference with Gary Oates on the Isle of Wight in the UK. I had a vision during the morning session, which repeated and continued during the afternoon session.

I'll start describing it and see if I go back into it while writing. [This did indeed happen.] I saw Jesus, bloody on the cross up above me. I put my hands on the cross. It was not smooth, but quite rough. His feet were above my eye level. I was a bit shaken at this sight.

According to Gary's teaching I paid attention to all my spiritual senses to note what was happening. I could see Jesus on the cross. I could feel the roughness of the wood. I could smell what was like dirt or dust along with some other "organic" smells. I then tasted salt on my lips; I appeared to be sweating. I could hear some quiet, murmuring voices.

As I stood below the cross, His blood began dripping on my arms. Jesus is in anguish. He grimaces in pain and lets out some quiet sounds—in agony. I am amazed as the blood continues to fall on my arms. It also falls on the back of my hands. I can feel the drops as they impact my skin. Jesus looks down at me and in the midst of His agony, smiles at me. You could see it took some effort.

"I love you," He says quietly, and with effort.

I look up to Him, not knowing what to make of all this. He now lets out a cry and grimaces in pain. I clasp the cross again. I know He needs to do this—and I know He's not really on the cross today, but nonetheless here I am, almost back in time seeing this.

I look down and see I'm wearing a rough fabric robe. There's a brown belt around my middle and I'm wearing sandals. I continue to hear the murmuring voices around me. One voice shouts out louder, but it is in a language I do not understand.

I now see a woman I seem to perceive is Mary under the cross. Her hands are trembling and she looks up, quietly sobbing as she beholds her Son. I see a man come up alongside her, trying to comfort her. I have a sense he's upset, but holding it in.

I look up and see a bolt of lightning in a dark sky, followed by a crack of thunder. Jesus dropped His head just as the lightning streaked across the sky. He was obviously gone. The wind is picking up; dust is swirling about. People begin to move away.

There is a deep rumble in the earth. Interestingly, I sense this rumble is somehow connected with the movement of Jesus' spirit. It's as if, wherever He has gone, the very movement—the very passing of His spirit has caused the earth itself to tremble.

The vision seems to end at this point, but I can very easily go back and see Jesus on the cross, his blood dripping on my arms. The drops falling on my arms is quite palpable.

I also see something I don't quite understand. When I look at both my forearms, each has a long mark, 6-8 inches in length. Both marks look as if they may have been placed there by a whip. Jesus' blood drips all around these marks.

Reflections afterwards:
I am reminded of something Paul said in Galatians 6:17, "From now on, let no one cause me trouble, for I bear on my body the marks of Jesus." I'm not yet certain of the entire significance of the marks on my arms, but will continue to meditate on it.

W. W. Wiersbe in the book "The Bible Exposition Commentary" remarks, "There was a time when Paul was proud of his mark of circumcision (Phil. 3:4-6), but after he became a believer, he became a "marked man" in a different way. He now gloried in the scars he had received and in the suffering he had endured in the service of Jesus Christ."

Sometimes during these experiences, I don't have to be specifically told something. Rather, I somehow sense what is happening, or sense its significance. It's as if the Spirit imparts knowledge or an awareness to me. It's very difficult to describe…but "you know that you know."

This happened when I heard the deep rumble within the earth. Just as a boat leaves a wake as it passes by, it was as if the very passing of Jesus' spirit through the earth caused it to tremble. It's one of those things that's interesting, for whatever it's worth…

To sum up, this was indeed a very impactful experience…and one I shall return and meditate on.

The Fire of Purity

I see lots of fire. Tongues of fire are leaping perhaps 15 feet into the air. Every so often there's a big flare-up with just a big mass of flames. Right now, the fire is raging. I can hear it roaring as it swirls about. I hear popping noises reminiscent of burning wood. I don't see any wood here, however. I sense these noises and pops have to do with the purification of that which is impure. The fire increases and becomes even more intense. The fire seems to be only in front of me, not beside or behind me. A big flare-up grabs my attention.

"Jesus... Holy Spirit, I just wait on You to show me what's happening here."
I see something moving about in the fire. It almost looks like arms waving about...but they are made of fire. I see now what looks like a figure made of fire, swirling about in amongst the flames. It bends, swoops, twirls about almost as if it is dancing. This continues for a little while.

Suddenly what looks like a man made of fire appears before me. He is glowing red and yellow...it's almost as if he is made of molten metal. Flames, perhaps 6-10 inches long occasionally flare up from various parts of his body. He is now holding up his hands, palms facing each other about 30 inches apart at shoulder height. Flames are shooting between his hands, almost like beams of energy.

"Come closer," he says. I move closer and he moves closer to me as well. He also appears to be wearing a robe of fire. "It is time," he says. "It is time for further purification. This may not be pleasant. But it will be worth it. I now baptize you with the fire of purity," he says while stepping closer.

He moves closer placing his hands on either side of, and about a foot away from my head. The fiery beam goes from one hand through my head to his other hand. However, I am now seeing myself in the vision. It's as if I'm outside myself observing what is happening. The vision of myself appears to be vibrating. The fiery beam becomes more intense. It permeates my body, which is lost in the glowing fire.

Suddenly it stops. The fire is gone. I'm back in myself. I see Jesus out in front of me. His hands still extended. Only now do I realize the figure was Jesus. He places His hands on my shoulders and runs them down my arms, as He smiles. "What you have seen is coming shortly," He says.

He then places what appears to be a glowing stone in my left hand. I lift it just a bit with my right hand and try to look better at it. "It is inscribed with your new name," He says. I would like to see it better, but cannot see the name, just the glowing stone. I continue to look... and now see some characters on it, but they are unknown to me.

I take the stone and clasp it in my hands. "Thank you, Lord," I say.

He replies, "Only I know this name. It is unique for you."

I stand amazed at all that has happened. The Lord continues to stand before me; His presence is so peaceful. It's almost as if peace is a substance that is part of His very being...
After a bit, the vision seems to be ending.

Reflections afterwards...
At first, I thought the fiery figure "dancing" in the flames was an angel. That could be. The "man" that subsequently appeared before me looked different, almost like he was made of intensely glowing, hot metal. Perhaps the first was a fire angel preparing the way, or announcing the One who was to follow. Initially I wasn't certain if the glowing man was Jesus or an angel. It wasn't until the fire vanished I could then see it was indeed Jesus standing before me.

As Jesus indicated, what I witnessed indicates something to come. Perhaps this is why I became an observer, watching what was happening to myself. It was not happening to me at the present moment, but will happen.

The glowing stone...with my name on it, jogs my memory. I distinctly remember seeing something like this in scripture, so I will try to find it...

It took a little searching, but I finally found it: "Whoever has ears, let them hear what the Spirit says to the churches. To the one who is victorious, I will give some of the hidden manna. I will also give that person a white stone with a new name written on it, known only to the one who receives it." *Revelation 2:17 (NIV)*

Interesting... a private name known only to the Lord and the one to whom it's given. Whatever was written on it was in an alphabet I did not recognize. I suspect in time my eyes will be opened to it.

All this continues to reinforce what I've been sensing in the spirit for some time. That is, I am currently in a time preparation. One cannot rush these things. In the Lord's timing, His purpose for my life will be fully revealed. In the meantime, my present purpose is to continue seeking, pursuing, and grabbing hold for the ride...wherever the Lord takes me.

Further reflections over a year later...
As I recently reread this experience something caught my attention: The "beam" between Jesus' hands passed through my head. I am convinced this is referring to a purification of my mind, my thoughts and how I think — a purification of my thought life. Initially the beam passed through my head, but then had an effect on my entire being. This illustrates what actually happens. As our thinking and thought life change, there is a ripple effect that permeates and affects our entire being. If we entertain the wrong kind of thoughts, that can have multiple negative effects, including physical effects. Likewise, pure and Godly thoughts can result in positive effects — spiritually, emotionally and physically.

I am reminded of Paul's remarks in Philippians 4:8 — "Finally, brother and sisters, whatever is true, whatever is noble, whatever is right, whatever is pure, whatever is lovely, whatever is admirable — if anything is excellent or praiseworthy — think about such things."

The Unveiling

I see a really skinny man. He has virtually no meat on his bones. He's not really emaciated, but very, very thin. Two angels appear on either side of him. The angel on the man's right places one hand on the man's right shoulder and then takes the man's right hand. The angel on the man's left does the same thing on that side.

I now see the man is dressed in a white robe, but it fits closely to his body, so one can see how thin he is.

The angels seem to be blowing on him; his robe moves about a bit. There is a very large pillar to the right and left of this scene. The pillars are very tall and seem to stretch into the sky. I'm now aware of a white staircase behind me, which stretches about the width of the pillars, perhaps 30 or 40 feet. The bottom of the staircase descends into clouds. There appears to be clouds on either side of this scene as well.

The angels continue to blow on the man and every so often a big puff of white fire travels up the man and disappears a short distance above his head.

My viewpoint is now further back, over the steps looking straight ahead. I can take in the whole scene; clouds on the outside, pillars just inside that and the man with the two angels in between and maybe 10-15 feet behind the pillars.

The puffs of flame get even larger. I can hear them as well. It reminds me of someone trying to start a gas fire…it suddenly puffs up, but then goes out. The puffs of fire get even bigger, encompassing the whole body of the man. But they do not stay lit.

The fire finally now remains lit. It starts at a small diameter at the man's feet, but completely envelopes him like a tornado, getting larger as it towers many feet over his head.

I now see the scene from a further distance. The angels are still blowing at the man who is encased in fire—but he can no longer be seen. The fire is huge, towering perhaps 50 feet or more into the air. Now the fire becomes even larger in diameter as the angels move back, but continue to blow. Bright flashes of light rise up quickly through the fire.

The fire is now huge. The angels seem tiny in comparison. The flames must be over 100 feet in the air and nearly 50 feet in diameter.

Now—suddenly—the fire goes out. The angels are no longer blowing. I see what looks like a pillar of carbon standing where the man was. In fact... it is the man. I can see a single eye opening, blinking. The angels come back in closer. They take the position they had before, each with a hand on the man's shoulder and each holding one of the man's hands.

"Lord, what's going on here? Am I going nuts?"

"Keep watching," a voice says.

I try to get in a little closer. I now see what looks like a tear coming out of the man's right eye. It rolls down his cheek and leaves a little trail of clean skin behind.

"Come here," he says to me. I find myself walking toward him. I stand about six feet away.
This is absolutely crazy. I now see what looks like a crown of thorns on his head. They appear nearly black as well.

"Lord, this really has me puzzled. I really need to know what's happening here."

The man now reaches his blackened hands out. "Take them," he says. I put my hands into the man's hands.

"Lord Jesus I just need to commit this to you. If this vision is of You, may it keep going. If not, I ask in Jesus' name it be removed." [I said this at the time because the vision seemed so incredibly outrageous. I wasn't convinced it was from the Lord.]

170

I now sense this man is the Lord. "Lord, what is happening here? I really need some revelation."

I now discover a cloth in my hand. I begin to wipe his face off and can see it much better.

"Keep going," He says.

It seems like all I need to do is think about it and more cloths appear in my hands as I need them. Some are wet with some kind of cleaning solution. I wipe Jesus down. This is just terrible…he's so full of black stuff. But I'm determined to get Him cleaned off. I take the wet cloths to His face and also clean off His hair. As I keep cleaning Him off, I'm seeing Him more as I have in previous visions…and not so thin as what I originally saw. He smiles at me as I continue my efforts. It just seems like such an overwhelming job.

"Lord, I don't know if I can ever get all this dirt off of You…it's all so much."
However, I know if I spend enough time at this, I can do it, but it's going to take some work and time.

"You're starting to understand," Jesus says as I continue cleaning.

"Maybe in part," I reply.

"Just continue to contemplate it," Jesus says. "I will reveal it to you. I'm pleased you stuck with this vision. I know you were tempted to just walk away from it."

"It's been hard, Lord. But I trust You."

He still has some smudges here and there, but puts His hands out again. I stop and take His hands.

"Just spend time with Me, He says." I continue to hold His hands.

"It wasn't easy for the prophets either," He says. "Many times during their visions, they just wanted to shut them off, because they seemed so bizarre. But they came to recognize the necessity of trusting Me and allowing them to continue. In some instances, they never understood the meanings of what they saw. Rather it was to be disclosed to those who followed. This was another lesson in trust. You have done well. Consider what you have seen."

Reflections afterwards:
This was all very, very bizarre. However, I can reflect on what I think I understand so far...
It is now obvious the very thin man I saw at the beginning was the Lord. However, *I had what might be described as a very distorted view of Him.*

Much in the middle of the vision remains mysterious at this point. However, I do sense something about the end. Even then, the view I had of Jesus was very distorted. It wasn't until I started working and cleaning Him off, that I recognized Him.

The fact is, unveiling Him took work on my part. I had to invest time and energy into it. Sometimes I think we look for easy, dramatic revelations from the Lord. However, when it comes to seeing Him as He really is, we have to be willing to pursue this. It takes time and effort, but He rewards us accordingly.

As we continue to pursue Him, our distorted perceptions of Him will give way to an understanding and realization of who He truly is.

The next day I continued to receive revelation pertaining to what I saw:

Regarding the fire: That was the burning of misconceptions. It took the angels multiple attempts to get the fire going. Perhaps this relates to stubbornness on our parts. When we really grab on to an idea, even if it's mistaken, it can be a difficult thing to change.

Regarding the role of the angels: It seems as if the angels were assisting in the burning of the misconceptions. We know they are assigned to minister and help us.

I did not start taking action until the angels were finished with their work. The Lord Himself actually prompted the start of my work in "unveiling" Him. He did this with a tear. I could see clear skin underneath. The need for me to get involved and start the cleaning process was instigated by this initial revelation.

So, what are the characteristics of a really thin man? One apparent trait would be a lack of strength and power. Of course, that is the opposite of Jesus. But think about this: When we fail to truly trust Him in difficult times, what do we *really* believe about Him? Do we *really* believe He is all-powerful, or not? Do we *really* believe He's going to take care of us? If we have doubts, it shows our picture of Jesus is, in fact, distorted. We may intellectually acknowledge Jesus is all-powerful, but nagging doubts prove we haven't yet *fully* believed in our hearts.

About the tear: His earnest desire is, for us to clearly see Him as He is...to understand and know Him as He really is.

Once the misconceptions were burned away, it became necessary to discover who He really is. This was signified by cleaning off the dirty soot of old beliefs, which distorted my view. This took a deliberate act of my will...and some determination.

When we truly understand in the depths of our hearts who Jesus is, it gives us absolute confidence — and peace — in the most difficult of times.

Defeating the Storms

I'm standing with Jesus at the edge of the surf. My back is towards the beach; Jesus' back is towards the sea. We're holding hands. I'm just spending time with Him.

The gentle waves wash in and out over my feet. I feel sand being washed over my feet. It moves back and forth with the waves. I find I must move my feet every so often. If I do not, they start becoming buried. It's a bit hard lifting them up because the vacuum wants to hold them under. When I pull them up, they leave holes behind in the sand. The waves quickly wash them in.

Interesting. I notice Jesus does not have to do this. He stands there; his feet always remain on the surface of the sand. It's almost as if gravity and the action of the waves have no effect on Him. Jesus smiles and seems amused I've noticed this.

"Is there some significance to this Lord?" He smiles and says, "Perhaps…just think about it."
I think to myself, "Perhaps indeed." I will of course meditate on it. I should have known better than to even ask such a thing, but it seems to be the way of things. I sense He's pleased with me however, as I am trying.

Some slightly bigger waves wash over us now, half way up my shins. The bottom of our robes are washed about. The force of the water and moving sand is much greater, but Jesus' feet remain on top of the sand.

A starfish is crawling along the bottom, comes to Jesus' left foot and starts to climb up His leg. It climbs out of the water, up His leg on top of His robe. Jesus takes His right hand and gently removes the creature, setting it down in the water to his right and it continues on its journey.

Of course, I wonder what is going on, but don't even ask. I'm sure He wants me to meditate on it. I now see a large whale some distance offshore swimming off to my left; the same direction the starfish went.

A mild wind springs up and blows from the right to the left; again in the same direction the creatures went.

I'm no longer holding Jesus' hands but have stood back a couple feet watching. A crab about 4 inches across crawls across the sand at the surf's edge. It too came from my right and is going to the left. The waves washing over it temporarily disturb its journey, but it rights itself and keeps on going. The wind continues to blow from right to left.

I now see some clouds in what was previously a blue sky...they too moving with the wind from my right to the left.

I'm standing back a bit further now looking over the scene. Jesus is still where He was, looking and smiling at me. The wind picks up a bit and I get a few bits of sand in my eyes. The wind continues to pick up. I walk back down towards Jesus and take His hands.

Suddenly all this stops. Everything is back as it was. The blue sky, the gentle waves...and the sand washing around my feet. Jesus is still standing there smiling at me. I'm aware of a bright, warm sun in the sky up at one o'clock, high. The heat from it feels nice. I hear waves gently washing in as the vision seems to fade.

I had no immediate answers what this was all about and was left very puzzled. However, this vision continued six days later...

I'm back on the beach looking at Jesus standing at the edge of the surf. I'm standing back a bit, taking the scene in. There's quite a wind blowing from the right. The sky is no longer blue but getting gray. The sky is appearing very dark to the right, as if a storm is approaching.
Jesus is still standing at the edge of the surf with His arms held out somewhat. A glow also surrounds Him as the surroundings become darker.

I hear the wind whipping up; swirls of sand blow about. It is now very dark off to the right. Lightning bolts flash about in the sky. It's odd, but it's almost like the storm possesses anger. I sense an evil overtone to the storm. Lightning bolts are flashing about in the sky over to the right. The sky is even more ominous…it's as if a powerful, dark whirlwind is swirling about in the clouds.

It appears threatening, but I'm not afraid. I'm reminded of the vision with the ugly creature blowing at the tree with birds taking shelter in it. The storm seems evil, but doesn't seem able to advance. Jesus remains solidly planted in the center of the vision, glowing in the midst of the gray fringes of the storm.

"You know what to do," Jesus tells me. Instantly and intuitively (from what I learned in another vision) I look out at the storm and say, "Be gone!" The storm collapses and shrinks. The sun and brightness return. However, there's a little remnant of a cloud over in the sky to the right. I say, "Hey, Jesus says be gone! Get out of here." The last of the cloud disappears.

"Very good," Jesus says. "You must remember to treat the storms in your life the same way. I will tell you how to defeat them."

"Thank you, Lord." I come down closer and take His hands.

"My peace I give to You. No one can steal it from you. Keep your eyes fastened on Me throughout your ordeals and you will always succeed. You are an overcomer in Me."

"Thank you, Jesus."

The creatures I saw in the last vision are coming back. Now they are coming from the left and moving back towards the right. I see additional creatures as well, such as fish swimming from left to the right.

I sense, "Watch the signs." The fleeing creatures were an indicator of the approaching storm before it arrived. At the time, I didn't know it was coming, but they did. They offered an advance warning.

A couple years ago, I received a prophetic warning from someone at a conference who didn't know me. A lady came up and said she saw me in a bullring along with the matador and picador. I was the bull and the matador was the enemy. The enemy sent the picador to throw some spears into and weaken me. She said there were two spears with what looked like sparklers on them. The intent was to weaken me after which the matador — the enemy — intended to come and take me out.

That word did not alarm me, but forewarned difficult times ahead. Within a few months, events conspired making it necessary for me to move into a new apartment. Simultaneously, events surrounding my job caused my finances to become critical. However, because of the warning received, I was psychologically prepared (as well as I could be) for those hard times. Important to note is this: The arrival of those difficult times did not take me totally by surprise.

This vision would suggest that if we are listening and attentive, God will at times forewarn us of coming attacks and difficult situations. And when the storm comes, He will instruct and lead us in the way to defeat it...or walk safely through it.

Thank you Jesus!

Confessing a Struggle

A few introductory remarks…
The issue I was struggling with at the time this experience occurred is not identified…nor does it need to be. One could plug just about any struggle into this scenario. Just because I've had a number of remarkable encounters with the Lord doesn't mean I'm somehow above the struggles common to others…quite the contrary! I've included this experience, so others can see both my struggle—and another side of the Lord as well. In many of my experiences, I've experienced the Lord's love, encouragement and even humor. However, as happens with any loving parent, there are times a more serious, even somewhat stern approach is needed. Yet regardless of His approach, everything the Lord does is couched in supreme love—that is always His motivation.

I'm again by the seashore at the surf's edge. Jesus is standing in the water, just a few feet in from the edge. My perspective is low, looking up, as if I'm on my knees. I place my hands into the water. The waves are very small, only 3-4 inches high. They gently wash in and out. I look up at Jesus. The sun is high, but somewhat behind Him, so His features are somewhat shadowed. He extends His hands towards me. I stand up and take them in my hands. His grip is strong. There's a feeling of safety in His presence.

"Are you ready?" Jesus asks.

"OK Lord," I respond.

Suddenly we are taken up into the air…and very quickly. My perspective is now outside myself. I can see Jesus and myself holding hands and rotating about each other. Although there still appears to be sunlight, the area around is quite dark…almost like we're in outer space.

For brief moments, I'm back inside myself holding Jesus' hands as we rotate about. But then at other moments, I see from an outside perspective.

I'm wearing my white robe. But it has a large black stain on it. It's located just below the left side of my chest.

"You see it," Jesus says. "Yes, I reply." I sense what it's about. Through my deliberate behavior, I've soiled it. I feel so terrible. I was given this white robe, but I've defiled it.

"Oh Lord, I'm so sorry."

"Are you really?" He asks.

I pause, not knowing how to answer. It's easy to say trite things.

"I do want to clean it, you know," Jesus says. "But if you continue to willfully soil it…" He doesn't finish the statement.

"What am I going to do about this Lord?" I ask. I don't want this spot on me. "What is the remedy?" I cry out.

"You must continue to seek Me," Jesus says. "You have been lax."

"I know Lord. I'm sorry. The things in my life, decisions need to be made…I've fallen into the very busyness of things I knew could happen. I knew better, yet it happened anyway. What's wrong with me?"

"You need to be washed. But I cannot do it apart from your cooperation. You MUST spend more time with me."

"I'm so sorry Lord. What's wrong with me?" I see the word "Discipline" spelled out before me.

"I know this is solvable. You wouldn't have brought me this far just to let me go. In fact, You promised never to do that. Lord, I need to relearn what I have lost. Help me Lord. I confess the need to have an undying, burning passion for You. A passion that will not die, that will not compromise."

Reflections some time later...
I am reminded of an illustration I've heard Gary Oates share several times. It is a pertinent reminder some issues in our lives can only be addressed by spending significant, quality time with the Lord:

A person makes a casserole, then serves it for a meal. The empty casserole dish is then set in the kitchen sink. The cook returns a few hours later, only to find the dish now encrusted with stone-hard "stuff" dried all over it. "Oh no!" the cook exclaims. "How am I going to get this clean?"

One option is to get a hammer and chisel and try to chip it out. Of course, this is pretty crude and could break the dish. But there is another option: fill it with water and let it soak. After some time has passed, one can hold the dish under a faucet and all that softened crud will easily slide out and simply wash away.

The same thing is true in our lives. By spending lots of time soaking in the Lord's presence, the crud in our lives will soften and can be easily washed away. There is no substitute for this. Yes, the Lord occasionally performs instantaneous works of healing, deliverance, etc. However, for most things, He desperately wants to spend time with us, softening our minds and spirits—and washing us with His Spirit. Impurities will yield and melt away...

But we must discipline ourselves in the midst of our busy lives to make room for Him. We cannot expect to become conformed to His image, without spending quality time with Him.

I must add that Jesus was in no way angry with me. He did however, state the truth in a direct fashion...and the whole experience caught my attention, which I'm sure is what it was designed to do! I am very thankful...the Lord's way is always the best way!

A Painful Lesson

I'm standing at the door. I push down on the handle and open it. I see diffuse light in the distance. I can see the ground in front of me and step forward. I'm a bit puzzled. I was seeing images of fire and felt a vision was coming. I wanted to be sure it was of God and put it into his hands. Although I've come through the door, everything seems indistinct and I can still get flashes of fire to the sides, almost on top of what I'm seeing. Perhaps my intent to go through the door is not what the Lord wants at the moment. There have been other times when I've gone straight into a vision without going through the door.

"Ok Lord, I was a bit apprehensive. I haven't met with you this way for so long. But I will back out of the door and let whatever You have take over." So I back out and shut the door.

"Ok Lord, I still see the areas of fire off to my side. I just give this to you."

I see towering areas of fire ahead; to the right and to the left. I now see what appears to be a pathway, perfectly straight going out into the distance. I see a white figure standing some distance away hovering over the pathway.

I approach. It's a pathway that appears to be bright yellow, like molten metal, but I can see it's made of something that looks like bricks, or perhaps plates of metal, the size of bricks. They fit very tightly together and are perfectly flat. Columns of fire continue to rise on either side of the vision. The walkway goes perfectly straight ahead. There's a glow of red in the sky and all around. The fire does not actually come up to the edge of the walkway, but remains some distance away, off to the sides. On either side of the walkway there appears to be some kind of berm, about 18 inches high, glowing a dull red. They have an appearance like mounds of lumpy soil piled up — or like coals — on both sides of the walkway.

I step on the walkway. There's a sizzling sound as I put my feet on the very hot surface. It hurts my feet and I step back off. The glowing white figure in the distance appears to be Jesus. I suspect He wants me to come to him. I thought I would just walk out to Him, but now I'm not sure. I've never been hurt before in a vision.

I stand and continue to look over the scene.

"Ok, Lord. If you want me to come to You, You'll have to provide a way." Suddenly what appears to be water emerges at the beginning of the path and starts flowing out upon it. There's quite a sizzling sound and lots of steam. The bricks are no longer glowing at the beginning of the path, but are still warm. I step again onto the pathway. Although the bricks are just warm, it's painful to step on them, as my feet are now very tender. It's as if I've burned my feet and they are now extremely sensitive to even a small amount of warmth.

I have a sense that the water would continue to advance along the pathway as I walked, but my feet hurt too much to proceed. I back up and remain in what seems to be cool grass before the edge of the path.

"Jesus, I need your help. I want to come to you, but it hurts to walk on these bricks."

I still see Him in the distance. Suddenly He's come to me — and appears right in front of me. He seems almost semi-transparent and all white.

"Take my hands," He says. I do so, and they become solid as I take hold. The rest of Him remains semi-transparent. This is all pretty strange.

As I stand there, it feels as if the blades of grass are moving around my feet. It's like they're alive somehow. I can now feel them tickling the bottom of my feet. Though my feet are still sensitive, the feeling of the cool, soft grass is nice.

Jesus blows down and across my feet; it feels very cool.

He says, "You were not prepared to come. You made assumptions and stepped forward before you should have."

"I'm sorry Lord. I've never been hurt before. You know I trust You to protect me."

"Yes, but you also have to listen," He replies.

"So now what Lord? Do you now want me to walk forward?"

"No. You've learned your lesson. I did indeed have provision for you to move forward. The water would have cooled the path as you came forward, just as you suspected. However, you were impatient and assumed I would protect you no matter what. You decided to walk forward before I actually called you to."

"I love you very much and will indeed protect you. But you must wait for my command, in places such as this. There is much happening you cannot see. Only I know the right time to proceed."

"Thank You, Lord." I just continue to spend time in His presence...and am grateful for this teaching...

Reflections afterwards...
It is late summer, but this is my first recorded vision of this year. I suspect I could have enjoyed many before this, but I was having a hard time getting settled down. It's been an extremely tumultuous year... I moved out of my apartment in the UK, changed jobs, moved back to Florida, was loaded down at work, suffered through a long and difficult business trip to Asia, endured yet another move from one apartment to another, and then on top of all this...my mother passed away. And that's only a partial listing. It's been difficult to just stop and spend significant, meaningful time with the Lord. After going through this period of turmoil, I finally "grabbed the bull by the horns," so to speak. I was determined I needed to spend a lot more time with the Lord...and listen to what He has to say.

I got glimpses earlier in the day of this vision. I've had others earlier this year, but with everything going on, I just didn't get into a position to receive. I decided, "No more procrastinating!" This time I was going to pursue it.

Because so much time had gone by, I was perhaps a little ill at ease and didn't allow things to flow as they should. I got in the way. As this vision started, I made an assumption. I went and opened the door into the spiritual realm I've gone through so many times before. I knew that was a safe route the Lord has sanctioned so many times in the past. I was even told I could come back through and visit whenever I wished.

However, it quickly became apparent, the Lord did not want me to come to Him that way. I finally backed out of the "safe route" I previously knew...and simply let the Spirit take me directly where He wished.

There have been times I've entered into the spiritual realm directly by Jesus' bidding (not via the door). In fact, all of my initial visions started that way. However, I was to learn an important lesson here.

I made at least two incorrect assumptions. First was my assumption to enter in via the door — from which I then backed out. Once I was in this vision, I also assumed I could simply step forward and go straight to Jesus. When going through the door, that was always possible. I had been invited to enter in that way — it was provided for me and came to know I wouldn't be hurt. I was therefore emboldened and confident.

However, this time I did not enter in via the door. I was there by invitation, but didn't seek the Lord's guidance. Instead I stepped out onto the path before being summoned — a big mistake.

This taught me we must not become overconfident when entering the spiritual realm. In this case, Jesus did not say a way for me hadn't been prepared. In fact, it later became apparent, a way to Jesus had indeed been prepared. Rather, Jesus said *I was unprepared.* I must now ask, in what way was I not prepared? I think perhaps in my attitude. I was in an unfamiliar place, jumped ahead and *assumed* I was to walk out to Jesus. It is now apparent I should have first inquired.

One thing in particular caught my attention when Jesus said, "You must wait for my command *in places such as this*." I am reminded of Peter and disciples struggling in the boat during the windy night. Though Peter was impetuous, he did not just jump out of the boat and start towards Jesus. Rather, he recognized he was in a highly unfamiliar circumstance and asked Jesus first. After Jesus bid him to come, Peter then proceeded.

Although this lesson was set in the spiritual realm, I believe it applies to our present lives as illustrated in Peter's example above. There are teachings out there that seemingly encourage people to "step out in faith" for anything and everything imaginable. In one sense that would seem admirable. However, we also need to seek the Lord and ascertain what *He wants* for us *right here and right now*. Our limited thinking and preconceived views can produce desires that may not match up with what the Lord has planned for us *at this moment in time*. Some people may think they are stepping out in faith, when in fact they are stepping out in presumption — without the Lord's specific guidance. (That's what happened to me above.) At the very least, this can result in disappointment. In worst case scenarios, it can lead to pain and suffering. For three or four days after my experience, my feet (in the spirit) remained tender and sensitive.

Especially in the spiritual realm, there is SO much we have yet to learn. We must never take anything for granted and keep our eyes fixed on Jesus...and His bidding.

Oh, and one last thing. Even here I witnessed the Lord's provision. Knowing ahead of time what would happen, He prepared that area of cool, soothing grass for me to stand in. I hadn't even noticed it until after I burned my feet and stood back from the path. Although I made a mistake, I wasn't punished for it. Rather, the Lord understood and provided comfort as I contemplated what had happened. He really is amazing and so considerate...unlike an earthly taskmaster.

"Everything I Make Is Pretty"

A few introductory remarks…
In comparison to most of my other experiences, this is a lengthy vision…and the reflections afterwards, even more so. Additional revelation came to me about six months after this experience and that is included as well.

It is very personal. Because of this and also because of its length, I questioned whether to include it in this book. I suspect some people might not find it of much interest. However, as I pondered this, I realized it could very well have value to others with similar struggles and decided to include it.

I have told the Lord in the past, to do whatever it takes to get me cleaned out, cleaned up and fit for His use. The fact is, if we are truly dedicated and give Him that kind of permission, He will stop at nothing to see it accomplished. When the Lord cleans us out, He *really* cleans us out! As the saying goes, He "leaves no stone unturned." Some of the stones He uncovered in this experience go as far back as is possible…

I've been wanting to return to the woodland garden. Jesus indicated it was a place of refreshment, which I could certainly use. I haven't been there in so long. I've been getting glimpses of the spring bubbling up…

My face is right over the bubbling spring. I splash some of the water into my face. In times past, the water has been either cool or warm, depending on my need. However, this is now most peculiar. It's hard to describe, but it's simultaneously warm and cool. In the natural, that's not possible. But here I can feel warm and cool at the same time. That's something really different. Also, as I've discovered in the past, I can place my face into the water and breathe it in. Unlike in the natural realm, you can't choke or drown in this water. One can just breathe it in. It feels so nice and smooth. I continue to splash the water in my face and breathe it in.

"I am the life," I heard the Lord say. I think to myself, "He is my life," as I continue to breathe the water in and out.

My attention is drawn to what appears like a patch of grass, an area perhaps about 15 feet across. I can't see any of the rest of the garden at this time…only the bubbling spring and this patch of grass about 8-10 feet away. I see what looks like dozens and dozens of small orange flowers coming up through the grass. They're not very big; sort of like large crocuses. I have a feeling these are related to the large orange flower I've seen in the garden before. Jesus said that big flower was some kind of "surprise." I still wonder what that's all about. I don't see that large flower at the moment, but have a strong sense these smaller flowers are somehow related.

Now Jesus appears in the grass to my left. As He faces me, He extends His left hand over the area of the small flowers. "Pretty aren't they?" He smiles and asks.

"Well, yes Lord; everything you make is pretty," I reply. My spirit *instantly* snaps to attention. I'm acutely aware there's something in what I just said. He stands there with His arms still extended and continues to smile at me.

"What was that?" He asks.

"I said, everything you make is pretty." I can tell He's pleased.

"You must never forget this," Jesus says. "Yes, everything I make is pretty."

Jesus continues, "I am peace. I am purity. Everything I make is filled with these attributes. Indeed, I am in all these things," He says as He motions over the grass and flowers. "And I am in you. Do not call unclean what I have made."

I'm a bit taken aback. "Are you referring to thoughts I harbor about myself," I ask.

"Yes, in part. But also in others."

"Lord, as I've looked at others recently, I've been trying to celebrate their uniqueness in you."

"Yes, but you have not been including yourself."

"Wow Lord. I'll have to reexamine myself. I thought I was making progress in this area."

"You have. But there are now deeper things to consider. Come close to me. You must embrace Me and as you do, embrace yourself. I have much more to show you."

Ok, Lord. I'm a bit puzzled by all this, but I submit myself to You.

The vision changes. I hear a baby crying.

"Congratulations. It's a boy."

I feel myself as being very small…in someone's hands.

[At this point I experienced what I can only describe as a word of knowledge within the vision.] A curse was put on me. I don't know by who, but someone or something cursed me.

"I will not permit this," the Lord says. "It wants to destroy you, but I will not permit it."

I now continue to see myself as very small, in someone's hands.

"Lord, I'm a bit puzzled by all this. Where do we go from here?"

"Come follow Me," He says.

I still see the hands holding me as a tiny baby…and wait.

"What would you like me to do?" The Lord finally asks. I'm puzzled by this. [I think I was waiting for the Lord to do something. However, He wanted me to do something…]

He finally says, "You must hold the baby."

I am now holding the baby, i.e., myself.

"Kiss him," the Lord says. I bring him close, and kiss his forehead. It's me. I begin to stroke him; he's cold. A blanket appears, and I wrap him in it.

"Hello Dougy", I say to myself — the baby. Suddenly as I say that — in a flash, I'm reminded of what we talked about earlier. Everything Jesus makes is "pretty." This is a pretty baby boy.

"You were deprived," the Lord says.

"Deprived? Deprived of what?" I ask.

"At the moment of your conception, at the moment of your birth, you were deprived of the love that was intended for you."

I must admit I don't really understand this. But I do sense a vacuum of some sort in my spirit around the time of my birth.

"I don't understand this Lord. I asked my mom about this a long time ago. She said I was very much anticipated and looked forward to by everyone."

"Not everyone," the Lord responded. "There were forces at work wanting to destroy you. But I have overcome those forces. They touched you and desecrated you. But I am here to tell you — you are fully restored. You might not think so. You still believe lies from the enemy, but I will expose these, reveal their falsehood and heal you. You are my blessed vessel. Although an attempt was made to dirty — even destroy the vessel, I can make everything clean. Indeed, I *have* made you clean, you just don't fully comprehend it yet. But you will. Come to Me, embrace Me and embrace yourself."

"Again, beauty and peace are part of my very nature…AND THEY ARE IN YOU…as I am in you!"

"Thank you, Doug for being patient."

"Lord, what else can I do? You have all the answers. You are the source of all knowledge. Indeed, you are my source for everything. I wait on You for your continued revelation."

I take the little baby in my hands and bless him and love him, in Jesus' name.

I now take him and place him in Jesus' hands…and just continue to rest in the peace of Jesus…

Reflections afterwards:
What I thought might be a simple visit to the woodland garden moved into something thoroughly unexpected. It did have me a bit mystified at first because I couldn't really see any of the garden, except the spring — at least initially. Then my attention was drawn to the pretty orange flowers. The color mystifies me because it's not actually a particular favorite of mine. Nonetheless, I've seen the large orange flower in the past, and now all these little ones.

The moment I said, "anything You make is pretty," I instantly knew was significant. It then led to an examination of myself as a baby. Considering I started in the garden, this was a totally unexpected turn of events.

Then there was this part of the conversation:
"*Do not call unclean what I have made.*"
I'm a bit taken aback. "Are you referring to thoughts I harbor about myself," *I ask.*
"*Yes, in part. But also in others.*"

I have struggled intensely with that very last statement. Grammatically, it doesn't seem to make sense. Had Jesus said, "Yes in part, but also thoughts you've harbored about others," would have made sense. Another alternative would have been, "Yes in part. But also the thoughts harbored by others." (In other words, the thoughts inside other people towards myself.)

Instead He said, "Yes in part. But also in others." Did I hear incorrectly? I must admit I wanted to go back and modify it, but couldn't…it's what seemingly came during the flow…as I heard it. There are also examples of things said in the scriptures that have left people perplexed. Perhaps the seeming incoherentness was by design. It has led me to spend a lot of time thinking about all this.

A short time ago, a friend in ministry was sharing how he has been regularly breaking off any curses or ill will spoken against him—but not just spoken words—*thoughts* against him as well. He said it has helped in dealing with some of life's challenges he's been facing lately.

Regarding the above, I now suspect both of my potential interpretations have merit. Perhaps the Lord was trying to drive home an important point via all the meditation I've been doing surrounding this.

Although the scriptures make it clear spoken words have power, thoughts can have great power, too. Jesus indicated that entertaining an adulterous scene in our minds would make us just as guilty as if we committed the physical act. That's power.

All this is interesting in light of where the vision went next. I don't know whose hands were holding the baby. I think possibly the doctor's. However, I had no sense he was responsible for the curse. In fact, that's why I said it was from someone or *something*. Indeed, Jesus said *"it"* wanted to destroy me. He also later referred to *"forces"* that wanted to destroy me. This suggests the curse may not have originated from some person, but from an evil spirit. Of course, it's possible someone may have inadvertently brought that spirit to the scene.

Regardless, this is not the first time Jesus has said the enemy wanted to destroy me. He has said this at least a couple times in previous visions. I am also reminded; this was prophetically spoken to me about 3 years ago. I was at a conference when a lady I did not know approached me. She said she saw a vision of me in a bullring, with me being the bull. The matador wanted to "take me out." The plan was to send the picador to first attack me. She saw two spears thrown into me…and they had what looked like sparklers on them. The plan was, after I was wounded and distracted, the matador (the enemy) would move in for the kill. This word did not frighten me, but rather I saw it as warning that some difficult times may lay ahead (which turned out to be quite true). I was later thankful to the Lord for the advance warning, as the ensuing difficulties did not take me entirely by surprise.

As I was holding myself as a baby, I was aware the Lord instigated this as a way for me to embrace myself for who I am. However, as I was doing so, the Lord spoke saying I had been deprived. *"At the moment of your conception, at the moment of your birth, you were deprived of the love that was intended for you."* Of course, both of these moments are major milestones in the life of new person.

At the moment of conception:
Perhaps when I was conceived, little thought was given to the creation of a living person, but instead centered on the sensual fulfillment of carnal desires.

At the moment of birth:
During my entire childhood, the lack of love, acceptance and positive, character building input from my father is something I'm well familiar with. A great deal has been ministered into this area over the years. I'm certain even my birth has been prayed into (and more than once) during ministry sessions. However, perhaps there remain issues surrounding my birth that still require attention.

I did ask my mother some years ago, how I was received as a newborn child. Was I accepted? Did people look forward to my appearance? Her response was quite positive. I was their first child. Furthermore, I was the first grandchild for both sets of grandparents. In addition, I was the first great-grandchild for at least two sets of the great-grandparents. So yes, my appearance was seemingly very much looked forward to by a lot of people.

However, the Lord specifically mentioned the time of my birth. It occurs to me, a newborn infant might be both startled and afraid during and immediately after the birth process. I remember as a child, I was very, very easily frightened, especially by rough physical activity. Did I receive the immediate comfort I required? How quickly was I placed in my mother's arms and how much time did I have with her? Was I whisked away for circumcision and how long was it before I returned to my mother? Alas, I just lost my mother only a few weeks ago...and those questions can no longer be answered.

In particular, where was my father at this time? Did he ever hold me? (Generally speaking, he rarely touched me.) Many questions, but no one is left to answer them. Perhaps they don't need to be answered. One thing is known: The Lord indicated some kind of love I required at birth was missing. There is no question there was a vacuum on the part of my father. However, *I never had a sense he didn't want me.* Nonetheless, he was a very disturbed person and really didn't know *how* to love anyone. The capacity simply wasn't there.

Additional thoughts and answers about six months later...
I was in church yesterday and we were singing the song "No Longer Slaves" from Bethel Music. As we were singing the following words I had a vision. I saw the Lord holding me in His hands...as a newborn baby. I instantly knew in my spirit it referred back to the above experience.

Chorus
I'm no longer a slave to fear
I am a child of God

Verse 2
From my Mother's womb
You have chosen me
Love has called my name
I've been born again, into your family
Your blood flows through my veins

Bridge
You split the sea, so I could walk right through it
All my fears were drowned in perfect love
You rescued me, so I could stand and sing
I am a child of God!

Chorus
I'm no longer a slave to fear
I am a child of God!

I was stunned by what I was seeing in the spirit...and simultaneously proclaiming with my lips. After the original vision, I said I didn't know whose hands were holding me. I speculated they belonged to the doctor who delivered me. However, I now know it was the Lord's hands.

Why didn't I know that at the time? Usually such knowledge is imparted to me in these visions. However, is this not true in life? How many times has the Lord been actively engaged in our lives, but we fail to recognize Him at the moment?

I also now know in the depths of my being, it was a spirit of fear that attacked me at my birth. As recorded in my earlier notes above, I was quite fearful as a child. I now know why. Where it came from, I do not know...and perhaps I don't need to know.

But what I do know is this: I once had a spirit of fear, *but Jesus has delivered me from it!*

I remember in an earlier vision where Jesus had showed me the abyss. At that time, I saw Him cast a spirit away from me. He said it could never come back and torment me again. Was that when this particular spirit was torn away and dispatched to the abyss? Possibly.

I find all this amazing and it continues to demonstrate how the Lord is actively working in my life — even when I'm oblivious to it.

God's Infinite Perception

I'm walking with Jesus along a country road. It appears to be a dirt road, but the road is a very light color, like crushed limestone. I see some open areas and trees scattered about. As we walk toward the west, the sun is very low in sky, a bit off to our left. Jesus is to my left and I walk by His side.

"I'm glad you're writing this down," He says.

I can hear the sound of our feet crunching on the dirt road under us. I sense some humidity and life in the air — the scents of growing plants and pasture. The sound of us walking on the road continues.

The sun is now just above the treetops in the distance. I sense a coolness in the air beginning to descend around us. I also hear crickets along the road. I now also hear some frogs; lots of them. This would suggest there must be water close by, but I don't see it. There's now quite a chorus of noises between many frogs and crickets.

The last of the sun is now just visible above the trees. We continue to walk…it's a bit cooler now. Jesus is just smiling, but not saying anything. He glances over at me occasionally.

"What is that noise?" Jesus asks. I reply, "It sounds like crickets and frogs."

"Yes; there's more," He says. "Listen carefully."

We stop walking and I look around. "Lord, I don't hear anything else."

He smiles, "There is much more. But you can't hear it all. Your hearing is limited. Mine is unlimited. I hear everything. I hear every blade of grass, every pebble and even the dust under our feet."

I'm not sure what to say.

"Even the sun," Jesus waves His hand in that direction.

This is amazing. I never thought of the sun making noise. Yet Jesus says He hears it.

"My hearing extends beyond what you can even imagine."

I stand somewhat perplexed. Jesus smiles at me. "You will understand someday. But for now, you must trust I hear what you do not."

Jesus and I face each other and take hands like we so often have before. "Just because I appear to you like this, do not think I am limited like humankind. What you are seeing is how I choose to reveal myself to you at the moment."

"Yes, Lord, I have seen you in other ways before. I remember that time you were so huge I was in the palms of your hands."

He smiles. "And it is well for you to remember."

"Jesus, can I ask what this place is?"

He replies, "It is yet another place I have prepared for you. Again, you will understand more as time goes by. Don't concern yourself with it, but rather, enjoy it." He starts swinging my hands. I kind of like it when He does that.

The sun has disappeared behind the trees. Mist appears in many of the open areas around us.

"Now, watch this," Jesus says. The sun suddenly rises backwards up the sky and nearly straight overhead. The temperature warms and we are suddenly in the middle of day.

"Ok, Lord, I know You can do anything; what is the point of this?"

"Don't put limitations on Me. What you just saw is impossible in the natural, but for Me, all things are possible…and effortless."

The sun beats down on us and I can now see what looks like wet areas around us. I wouldn't describe this place like a marsh. However, there are numerous small areas perhaps ten feet across with shallow water in them. The ground is dry in between. I hear a breeze rustling the leaves and plants.

"You heard that," the Lord said.

"Yes," I replied.

"So did I, but I always hear more — much more."

This is all a bit mystifying. Jesus smiles at me as He often does when my poor little head tries to process everything. "Don't strain yourself," Jesus laughs in jest.

"Ok Lord; I thank You for all this."

We now start to walk back in the direction from which we came, the sun still overhead.

"I am in complete control," Jesus says.

I think to myself that's obvious, but how often do I really comprehend that?

Jesus swings my hand as we walk. "You would have missed all of this had you not written it down," Jesus says. "You must do more. Much more."

"Thank you Lord."

I now see myself with Jesus walking down the road. It's as if I'm looking through a hole, or portal. It grows smaller and I can't see it much anymore. I feel sad. But I'm certain I'll be going back.
Now I've got to ponder what all just transpired...

"I am always here with you. I will help you understand. Just spend time with Me."

"Thank you Lord."

Reflections afterwards...

Interesting... At both the beginning and end of the vision, the Lord mentioned how important it was I wrote everything down. I'm almost certain I would have had many more encounters with Him this year — especially recently, had I only sat down and quieted myself before Him. Now that I've been working full time again, it's been a real challenge to do so. Traditionally the most fruitful times I've had with the Lord have been in the evenings, an hour or two before going to bed. But I have to admit, in recent times it's often been less than an hour. I've also found myself more tired than I used to be late in the evening. The fact is, I haven't been giving the Lord enough quality time.

This time however, I came to him very much earlier in the evening, and I can tell the difference.

I was aware I was seeing, hearing, feeling, and smelling the environment around me. I had a sense part of this vision was to exercise my spiritual senses. But there was obviously a message too.

I was intrigued with the emphasis on what the Lord hears. Since these visions began, I've been concentrating so much on seeing. Although I've been aware of the necessity to experience everything (i.e. with all the senses), I guess sight has been my principal focus. It's also perhaps the most difficult for me. However, this vision would suggest everything is perhaps of equal importance. I suppose God's communication knows no bounds.

In fact, as I ponder this, it occurs to me that for God, hearing and seeing are perhaps — in a manner of speaking — one and the same thing. Let me explain...

Human hearing detects physical vibrations within a range of 20 Hertz to 20 kiloHertz. Vibrations exist below and above that, but we can't hear them. To our hearing, they are "invisible."

Our eyes also allow us to detect much higher frequencies in the electromagnetic spectrum — what we call light. I did some research into this. At the low end of the spectrum is red light at 430 trillion Hertz. The upper end of the spectrum is blue light at 750 trillion Hertz. However, this is just a tiny window of the electromagnetic spectrum. What we call electromagnetic waves technically begin at a few Hertz and extend out to at least 3 billion-billion Hertz as gamma rays. So again, our eyes see only a *very tiny* slice of a much greater reality.

And just how tiny is that slice? Visible light only accounts for *one-thousandth of one percent* of the entire electromagnetic spectrum — or 0.00001 percent! Another way to put it — even those with the best eyesight are still 99.99999% blind to the *physical* realities around us!!!

And if we are that blind in the physical realm, what of the spiritual realm??? It brings further insight to what Paul said in 1 Corinthians 13:12 —
"For now we see through a glass, darkly..." (KJV),
"We don't yet see things clearly. We're squinting in a fog, peering through a mist." (MSG)

However, God "sees" literally everything! Because we are finite, we talk about our five senses — which are also finite — and which together give us a very limited picture of what exists around us. However, God's perception knows no limits. Our senses perceive only little bits of reality. However, because God's senses have no bounds, they all blend together in what we might describe as "infinite perception." This is why I said, for God hearing and sight are actually part of the same thing...His infinite perception. He sees, hears, feels, tastes, smells everything *all at once and to beyond all limits*. It was amazing when the Lord says he even hears the sun...something well beyond our perception. He said He even hears the dust on the ground, something we can't even imagine.

Just to drive home the point, Jesus took note when I heard the leaves rustling in the wind and added He hears so much more.

Jesus then does something He's done before — something impossible in the natural. In this case the sun traveled backwards up into the sky. He then reinforces the experience by reminding me not to put limits on Him and that He is in control.

At first, it was almost like two seemingly unrelated elements were presented in this vision. First, God's infinite perception of everything... and second, the fact He's in complete control of everything. Obviously, there is a connection here.

So, I have a feeling there will be more to ponder about all this...

"I Give Abundantly"

I've been getting glimpses of Jesus in front of what appears to be a huge waterfall…

Jesus is standing in front of a huge waterfall. It must be many hundreds of feet across. I can see the water coming over the top, but it falls and disappears into mist below. I can now see Jesus and I hovering in the air in front of the falls.

It makes a huge thundering noise…an enormous noise. Jesus smiles at me as I'm taking it in. I don't seem to be able to see anything to my sides or behind me. The focus is the massive waterfall with Jesus in front of it.

I now notice I can feel mist wetting my skin. Despite all the thundering power, the peace of the Lord permeates my senses and spirit.

Jesus now appears smaller…further away from me and then nearly vanishes into the falls. I remain where I am just taking it all in. I can't see Him at the moment.

"Would you like to join me?" I hear the voice of Jesus asking.

"Sure, Lord," I reply.

Suddenly I'm sucked into the falls. Thundering water is everywhere and it's darker in here. But now I see Jesus just back outside the falls. I float back out to meet Him. I'm sopping wet.

What was that all about, Lord?" I ask.

"You just experienced a baptism" He replies

"A baptism?" I ask again.

"When I baptize, I don't give just a little. I give abundantly, thoroughly, completely. You cannot remain dry when I baptize you." Jesus says.

"What kind of baptism was this?" I enquire.

"It is what you need at the moment, including a baptism of peace." I do sense His peace around me.

Jesus continues, "People talk about baptism in the Spirit and water baptism. These however, contain just a very small measure of what I have for you. If you become fixated on a single thing, or experience, you can become oblivious to the fact I have so much more to give. Each experience is a stepping-stone. But you are not to remain in the same place. You are to take one step at a time, from glory to greater glory. I have much prepared for you. This waterfall represents but a small trickle compared to what is waiting for you, but you must pursue it…you must pursue me. As you do, you will find my resources and blessings to be inexhaustible."

I continue to look at the massive waterfall. And according to the Lord, this is just one trickle?? I remember Him telling me previously, not to limit Him.

"Lord, it occurs to me, I may be limiting you in ways I haven't yet identified. Can you show those to me? Can we work on those?"

He replies, "That is my very intention, but you must be willing to proceed."

"I am willing, Lord. You know things are hard for me sometimes, but I do want to learn and give it a try, so to speak."

Yes, you are willing, but you are not always aware. Your awareness of what I have for you will increase as you spend more time with Me. That is paramount."

"Yes, Lord. It's so hard right now, working full time again. I not only need to spend more time with You, but I somehow must also set time aside for proper, physical exercise. I want to do these things Lord, but I could use Your wisdom in learning how to manage my time better."

Jesus smiles and laughs, "You shall learn. We'll work on it together."

"Thank you, Lord."

I'm still hovering out in front of the waterfalls with Jesus. I notice I'm wearing my white robe and ring of gold on my head. "I really need to be cognizant of this so much more often," I muse to myself.

"You will," Jesus says. "Again, this too will come as you spend more time with Me. Your perception of yourself and what's around will change as you do so. As you spend more time with Me, your perception will be filtered by My Holy Spirit. He will illumine what you see and hear in new ways."

"Thank You Jesus."

I just continue to praise and worship Jesus in front of the falls…

Reflections afterward…

Today I acted on this vision as soon as possible. I began to see glimpses of the Lord in front of the waterfall last night before going to bed. I told the Lord I was determined to pursue it. I didn't let it out of my mind. The next morning as I prepared for work, it was there. I thought about it numerous times as I worked throughout the day. I was determined I would not let the recent pattern of missing these visions occur again!

Therefore, after arriving home from work, I immediately had a quick evening meal…and afterwards sat right down to meet with the Lord. Giving Him this quality time immediately after the responsibilities of the day were finished was very productive.

"You Cannot Ask Too Much"

After arriving home today, I took a shower during which I started to see Jesus sitting in a boat....

I'm sitting with Jesus in a boat. I see the water out of ahead of us beneath a very orange, late afternoon sky. There are few thin clouds; a few which filter down the strength of the sun. Jesus is in the front of the boat, sitting and facing me. He's leaning towards me with His arms crossed and resting on His left knee. He's smiling at me.

I can now hear the water lapping against the boat. Both Jesus and I are wearing robes that are light in color and made of a coarser fabric. It's by no means uncomfortable and seems to fit the rest of the rustic image around me. The boat appears to be a very rough, hewn wood and grayish in color. There are cracks here and there and the impression is it's quite well worn.

I just sit with Jesus.

After a bit, I extend my hands out towards Him. He breaks into a bigger smile and takes my hands. I look down at my hands...being held by the Son of God...what an honor. And I have a strong sense He really wants to do this. His desire for us is greater than we can imagine.

"That's true," says Jesus out loud. "You must tell people this. It is your mission. I love them more than they can possibly know, just as I love you more than you can possibly know. Your spirit is not great enough to contain all the love I have for you. I run over with more and more and more. I cannot be exhausted."

"Look at me," Jesus says. I look up again and see a great smile on His face. "I have so much more for you. Yes, I've said that before, but it is worth repeating. You cannot exhaust Me. You cannot tire Me out. You cannot ask too much." "Be blessed."

I just enjoy being with Jesus, the sun still behind and the waves lapping at the boat...

Reflections afterwards…

I had a sense from the start; Jesus did not want to take me anyplace. Rather He simply wanted to spend time together. The scene was amazingly peaceful.

The Big Fish

I'm in the boat again with Jesus, just like yesterday. In fact, it's as if we've never parted. Everything looks the same; Jesus is still in the same position.

I just relax with Him. I can hear the water lapping up against the boat.

Suddenly I hear what sounds like a great splash over to my right. Water comes down and lands on me. Jesus starts to laugh. "You didn't see that coming, did you?" He asks.

"No, Lord. What was it?

"A great fish." He says.

I hesitate and wait a bit, not certain what to say or what to ask.

But Jesus says, "Go ahead and ask. It's OK."

"I must admit sometimes I'm not sure when to say something and when not to," I reply.

"There must be no barriers between us. If you have a question, by all means ask. Remember, I am not like an earthly father who can become impatient. I am always happy and willing to answer your questions."

"Ok Lord." "So, what's with the big fish?" I finally ask.

"Ha, ha…that is your meal!" Jesus enthusiastically replies.

"My meal?"

"Yes, your meal. See…" Jesus waves his left hand in the general direction behind me and to my right.
I look and see we are very close to shore — perhaps 15-20 feet. There is a sandy beach and a charcoal fire set up. There appears to be a large, crudely made grate of some kind over the fire. The fish is so large it extends beyond the edge of the grate three or

four inches both at the head and tail. The whole complete fish appears to be over the fire. The fish could easily be 3 feet long.

I get out of the boat...the water is quite shallow...and I make my way ashore. Jesus gets out of the boat and pulls it behind Him to shore. He pulls it up a few feet onto the beach.

"Have a seat," Jesus says, which seems a bit odd as there are no chairs. I sit down on the sand. This is most interesting, because I'm not used to sitting like this. In a sense, it's a bit awkward. In the physical I was born with skeletal defects that do not permit me to sit on the ground...at least not like this with my feet crossed. I'm not at all uncomfortable, it's just that I'm not used to being in this position. I sense that Jesus knows these thoughts.

"Have a piece of fish," Jesus says. This is another "no-no" in the natural, because I'm allergic to many kinds of fish. However, I'm certain this will not harm me. I'm initially at a bit of loss however, because we have no tableware to eat with. So, I grab the middle of the fish as best I can and pull some meat away from the body. It comes away easily and must be very tender. I'm looking for bones, but don't see any. I now take the piece of fish and start eating it.

"Ha, ha," Jesus laughs, "I've been waiting for a long time for you to do this."

I'm a bit bewildered.

"When you first started experiencing Me in these visions, could you have done this?" Jesus asks. I'm not altogether certain I know what He's referring to. Some of my very first visions involved eating.

"Think and ponder it," Jesus says. "There is meaning here, you just need to discover it...and discover it you shall."

I get a sense this is the end for the moment...and it's time for some pondering...

Reflections afterwards:
Ugh. Why do things have to be this difficult sometimes? I think I will look through some of my initial experiences again. But before doing that, I'll make some initial observations…

As is frequently the case in these visions, the completely unexpected—and sometimes seemingly bizarre suddenly happens. The vision started out peacefully enough; it was a continuation of the previous experience. I thought I might just sit a while and enjoy Jesus' company. But then came that big splash.

Sometimes I'm not certain whether to say something right away, or not. I tend to wait and see if Jesus might offer anything. However, there are times when He is actually waiting on me. Perhaps some of my hesitation comes from my respecting Him…and not wanting to do something inappropriate. However, if I'm honest with myself, I wonder if maybe there isn't a touch of fear there too. I think this is the reason for His response, "Remember, I am not like an earthly father who can become impatient. I am always happy and willing to answer your questions."

If I, like a little child am stepping forth with the best of intentions, Jesus has no reason to become impatient. In fact, impatience is a manifestation of our carnal nature, something Jesus does not have.

I also understand when He says, "I am always happy and willing to answer your questions." If we're seeking to the best of our ability, our Heavenly Father will honor that. There are times of course, when the Lord may choose not to answer our questions—at least immediately. He always does what is best for us at the moment. Sometimes I think we can get so busy asking "Why, why, why," we don't pause long enough to discern the answer. In that scenario, the seeming lack of answers might cause us to slow down, spend more time and contemplate with Him.

How a person answers a question, can often be affected by their mood at the moment—how well they slept the previous night, or perhaps how well they like the person asking the questions.

However, God's responses are always motivated by love and what's best for the person...period.

The charcoal fire on the beach reminded me of Peter's experience when Jesus reaffirmed him. Perhaps I should read that account again as I ponder this experience.

Something occurred that's happened before in a vision...where I was able to do something I couldn't ordinarily do in the natural. The fact I could sit comfortably on the ground, was noticeable. In the physical, I have congenital defects in my legs preventing me from sitting easily on the ground. But in the spirit, I had no such limitation. Furthermore, in the physical, I'm allergic to many kinds of fish. But not in the spirit!

However, as I started eating the fish, Jesus then laughed and said, "I've been waiting for a long time for you to do this." That's where things start to get mystifying. He then asks, "When you first started experiencing Me in these visions, could you have done this?"

Done what?? What have I done that I couldn't or didn't do at the beginning? I must admit, this all seemed so bizarre I was wondering if this whole thing simply wasn't my own mind rambling away. However, I did let it run to completion. I've learned I need to do this and trust the Lord will make sense of it all in time.

I've been looking over earlier visions to get an idea what Jesus meant. The following are some general observations:

As noted, I did several things in the spirit that would otherwise not be possible in my natural body...and perhaps most notably, doing them *without hesitation*. I think the "without hesitation" is the important part, and perhaps speaks to following:

In early visions, I generally waited on Jesus to provide instructions for nearly everything I did. I've noticed I no longer wait for guidance regarding every single detail. It's a bit hard to put into words. I would describe my interactions now more like those of a mature person instead of a child, whose hand must be continually held and guided. Typically, one must explain everything quite clearly to a child. Children usually can't anticipate, process and understand things the way an adult can.

In my earliest visions, when Jesus offered me food, he also handed it to me. However, in this situation once the food was offered to me, I took the initiative, reached out and helped myself. Perhaps my willingness to step out and act (without explicit instruction) is what Jesus was commending.

When Jesus gave us the great commission, He did not spell out in great detail precisely how it was to be done. He simply said, "Do it." I believe He wants us to take some initiative, step out and get the job done. Of course, the Lord never intended we do *everything* ourselves. That's why He sent us the Holy Spirit to help. And that's why we need to remain sensitive to His leading.

However, there appears to be an increased awareness today regarding God's desire to partner with us in doing His work. For example, the Lord could easily evangelize the whole world by Himself. Instead, He has chosen to partner with us in seeing that work accomplished. He has not given us a highly detailed blueprint and set of instructions. Rather, He expects us to utilize the creativity, talents, spiritual gifts and resources He's given us to further His work. And like a loving Father, He is always by our side ready to lend a helping hand and guidance when needed. But I also believe He is overjoyed when He sees us taking the initiative, stepping out and utilizing what He has already given us.

"You Are Clean"

Today at church I had a vision while taking communion. We each took a piece of bread and dipped it into the common chalice of wine. I did so, but was not in a hurry to take it. Instead, I sat down, held it and was contemplating its meaning.

I was asking the Lord for further revelation regarding the power of His blood... I then began to see Him in my mind's eye. He was fully robed and had what looked like a sheet of fabric wrapped around His neck, partially over His shoulders and hanging down just past His waist.

The ends of it, especially the right side (from His viewpoint...and that's where my attention was focused) was saturated in blood...His blood.

He came to me, took the wrapping saturated with His blood and began to wipe my face with it. I was very moved as this went on for a few moments. He then took the end of the sheet, held it over my head and began to wring it out...drops of His blood fell on my head. I was pretty overwhelmed...almost stunned by the experience.

The people around me had finished and were now singing a song — but I couldn't get up. I was too immersed in what was happening. Finally, the pastor got up and started his message, so I began to focus on that, but knew I had to write this down and further contemplate it.

Later in the evening...
I can still see Him in front of me, washing my face. He's smiling.

"I never stop washing you. I wash you even when you are unaware of my presence, but I am there doing this always."

I don't know what to say. Every so often, He scrubs just a little bit...it's almost as if He's spending time removing blemishes.

"And so I am," He says. "This is part of your journey to holiness, to purity. You are already clean."

"You've told me that before, Lord. But if I'm already clean, why are you still wiping me off?"

He smiles. "It's because you *think* you are dirty."

"Is this all tied up in the lies of the enemy you've mentioned in the past?" I ask.

"Yes, it is. My way is the path of holiness; you know that. But you continue to soil yourself."

"I don't deny that, Lord. But how can I be dirty and clean at the same time?"

"The dirtiness is in your thoughts. I have made you clean."

I start seeing a picture. I see what looks like a glass jar of pure, white milk. However, my hands smear the bottle with black dirt. It's an illustration.

Jesus explains, "The pure white milk is you. The container is your body and thoughts. Although the milk is pure, that purity is obscured by your actions. However, I am always here to help clean the bottle off. We will work together to do this—our hands together. You must help."

"Ok Lord, I'll try. In other words, you're saying I must put forth an effort."

"Yes."

He continues, "I am always standing here with my blood cleaning you. But the purity I've placed within you won't be seen until you stop adding more dirt. Once you stop, and allow me to finish the job, the real you...and the purity I've placed within you will be visible for all to see."

"Thank you Jesus."

Reflections afterwards...
This vision addresses what some find a puzzling dichotomy seen in the scriptures regarding our salvation. On one hand we read verses that suggest our salvation is a finished experience. And yet other scriptures paint a picture of a continuing process that is not yet completed.

These verses seemingly suggest a finished experience:

"And God raised us up with Christ and seated us with him in the heavenly realms in Christ Jesus..." Ephesians 2:6

"Therefore, if anyone is in Christ, the new creation has come: The old has gone, the new is here!" 2 Corinthians 5:17

"When he had received the drink, Jesus said, 'It is finished.' With that, he bowed his head and gave up his spirit." John 19:30

Some have taken such verses out of the context of the rest of scripture, essentially insisting we are already entitled to 100% of the benefits of Christ's atonement—right here and now. However, we must also consider verses like these...

"But we have this treasure *in jars of clay* to show that this all-surpassing power is from God and not from us." 2 Corinthians 4:7 NIV (Italics mine.)

Following that verse, Paul launches into a discussion describing how we are still living in our old "tents," and waiting to be clothed in the new, incorruptible tents. He also discusses this in Romans 8:23-25 where he says: "We ourselves, who have the firstfruits of the Spirit, groan inwardly as we wait eagerly for our adoption to sonship, *the redemption of our bodies...* Who hopes for what they already have? But if we hope for what we *do not yet have*, we wait for it patiently." (Italics mine.)

What is it we are yet waiting for? "The redemption of our bodies." So yes, the new creation has indeed *arrived*, but it's still being revealed a step at a time, so to speak. There's more we have yet to receive.

God promised and gave the land of Canaan to the Israelites. But just because God "gave" it to them, does that mean they *literally possessed it all at once?* No. There was a process; they laid hold of the promised land a piece at a time…and as God led them.

I must admit I've been a bit puzzled by the fact that on one hand God calls me pure, yet at the same time I still struggle with imperfections…and in worst case scenarios, sin. The illustration the Spirit gave me sheds light on this…along with the scriptures I've recalled above.

The "milk" is the real me—my spirit. Jesus' blood has purified my spirit. However, my spirit is still trapped in what Paul calls the old "tent," with its rips, tears and imperfections.

→ *Here however, is something of particular interest:*
Jesus said the bottle represented both my body *and my mind.* This suggests there are elements within "our minds" that are inextricably intertwined with our flesh. In a sense, this should come as no surprise. Drugs for example, can have adverse effects on our body…which can then also affect our mind.

However, it is also true—what is happening in our spirit can also affect our mind. Many will testify how the peace of God imparted to their spirit, can work its way into their mind and subsequently into their body.

This gives new impetus to the concept, "the mind is the real battleground." And it should therefore come as no surprise the mind is the primary arena the enemy works in—with deception being his primary weapon. And stop and think about it… *Deception is not a function of the body, nor of the spirit. Rather deception is completely within the realm of the mind.*

Jesus has purified us in spirit, but He desires that purity to work itself out through our minds and our bodies. Only then can we find true fulfillment in Him. The enemy of course wants to stop this. The whole purpose of the enemy's deception is to keep the purity of the spirit trapped within us…rendering us immature in thought and ineffective in action.

I need to truly believe who Jesus says I am. By doing so, the deceptions of the enemy can be neutralized and rendered impotent. I must choose *who to believe* and *what to confess* — what Jesus says, or what the enemy says.

The Time of Preparation

I was rereading one of my experiences in the beautiful valley with the stream. Everything in that place was symbolic. The stream was the stream of my spirit...mingled together with the Spirit of the Lord. I have now once again returned...

I'm much further down the stream than I've ever been before. The grass is taller, lush green with many wildflowers among the grasses. It's a gorgeous scene. The sky is bright with light overhead. I can hear the sound of the water flowing. I know the Lord is with me, though I can't see Him.

Instead my attention is drawn to the stream...it's wider here and flowing into the sea. (And I sense this "sea" is actually fresh water.) The luxuriant grass and wildflowers grow right down to the very edge of the sea. There is no small beach, or gravel border area of any kind. I've never seen anything quite like this in the natural world.

"This is your future," the Lord says. "The sea is the body of believers. This is the end of your journey of preparation. You will be released into the body with others to minister. You will flow together with them."

I see and understand. The journey of my life began at the source of the stream. To recount from my earlier experiences, it was a small spring of cold water quite some distance from here. That area was semi-dry and apparently not very fertile. Everything looked old and tired, like vegetation in very late summer. It represented the world my parents brought me into. The water of my spirit was cold and sterile as it came up from the ground and meandered away.

But then the little, cold stream flowed into a big red pool of warm water. That's when I encountered Jesus. Red represented Jesus' blood and the water His Spirit. The cold water of my little stream joined and flowed into Jesus. Our spirits mingled together and we flowed together out into the new stream...and into what would become a greener, lusher land.

But the stream was initially compromised. There were both cold and warm currents flowing within the stream. It's as if these currents flowed alongside and around each other — the water was not yet 100% perfectly mixed, through and through.

There were also occasional rocks in the streambed representing impurities in my life. They were stuck in place and impeded the free flow of the water. However, I had the ability to dislodge these and allow the water to flow freely. But it involved seeing the rocks, making a choice to do something about them, and then acting to dislodge them. The power behind the stream (the Spirit) then washed them away.

There were also black rocks in the landscape around the stream. I now understand they represented impurities, primarily in the environment around me. Curiously, I never did anything to clean these up. The Lord apparently took the responsibility of doing that.

The further downstream I went, the fewer the black rocks and lusher the landscape. The path of the stream represents my journey through life.

Now where the stream flows into the sea, I see no black rocks, just beautiful, verdant landscape. The Lord said this represented the end of my time of preparation. It's still in the future — but that time is drawing nearer. I would be released into whatever ministry the Lord has prepared for me...and I would flow together with others ministering in the Body.

Now, just because I didn't see any black rocks where the stream entered the sea doesn't imply I would be "perfect" in every sense. I don't believe that for one moment!! However, what I believe the Lord was showing me was this: Personal obstacles potentially impeding my future ministry (whatever that is) had been removed.

When I looked out into the sea however, I was a bit disturbed. I sensed movement out in the water…sharks! I was immediately reminded of Acts 20: 29-31, *"I know that after I leave, savage wolves will come in among you and will not spare the flock. Even from your own number men will arise and distort the truth in order to draw away disciples after them. So be on your guard!"* And 1 John 2:18-19, *"Even now many antichrists have come. This is how we know it is the last hour. They went out from us, but they did not really belong to us. For if they had belonged to us, they would have remained with us; but their going showed that none of them belonged to us."*

This was a bit sobering, but in retrospect, not surprising. After all, Paul said we need to be on guard. The body of Christ (the church) should be safe place. But the enemy sends in his agents attempting to deceive, divide and scatter the flock. Therefore, we need to be vigilant.

I now stand back, look at all this and shake my head in astonishment. For me to be thinking in terms of symbols and abstractions is unprecedented. In high school, I greatly disliked English literature classes. I especially despised one particular class. The teacher had us reading material written in various "levels of abstraction."

I seem to recall a story about a man walking through the woods and observing things in the forest. The teacher then enquired, "But what does this story *really* mean? What is the author *really* saying?" Students would come up with surprising "interpretations." But I was *totally* lost.

I did possess a significant, artistic sense. However, in the realm of communication, I was 100% left brain. I could only communicate in logical, precise terms. If a story was about a man walking through the forest, that's what it was about. Period. If the author was trying to say something totally different, why not clearly say what he meant? If the man in the story is not looking at "trees" but actually talking about people, why not say so? Why express things in such a way people can't readily understand them? Not surprisingly, the teacher did not appreciate my line of reasoning…and needless to say, I did not do well in his class!

Here I am decades later, and the Lord is communicating with me via parables—of all things! Ugh! Now since He has chosen to do this, I've been forced to admit there must be *something* valuable in this sort of communication. When I started experiencing visions with more abstract elements, I *slowly* began to understand there was genius behind this approach.

When Jesus addressed the crowds, He could have chosen to teach using only "plain language." However, in that scenario, His teachings would have been instantly interpreted through people's intellects. Anything learned this way is filtered through our preconceived notions and rigid ways of thinking. By teaching in parables, Jesus forces us to ponder. We are forced to look beyond the quick, simplistic answers that often just pop up in our heads.

Pondering takes time. I also believe this is one way the Lord entices us to spend more time with Him. Meditating with Him allows His teaching to sink into our spirits—to sink in beyond the limitations imposed by our often, simple-minded intellects. Truths that take root and reside in our spirit can in turn, work themselves out through our entire being.

A Heart for The Lost

I was rereading the experience I had two years ago when Jesus showed me the abyss. During and after reading it, I kept seeing glimpses of what appeared to be the same place…an occasional tongue of fire, the simmering magma below…darkness and black rock surround the periphery. I now also hear a deep rumble like that of fire in a great furnace.

However, something is different… Occasionally I hear what sounds like a scream. And now there's more of them—a great many screams. I see what appear like human bodies falling from above…but they are not physical bodies. I can see through them…they must be human spirits falling into this place.

When I look up, I see an area of light above. The human spirits are coming…falling out of the light and into the magma below. It's horrible. There are so many of them; it's like rain falling from above.

"This is not what I intended." The Lord says soberly. He is standing by my right side.

We are together on a ledge, overlooking what is happening. The human spirits continue to rain down from above.

"They have made their choice. I did not want this to happen. They have done this to themselves," the Lord says with emotion. I can see He is disturbed.

"No!" he says. "They would not listen!" He puts his face into his right hand. "I paid it all. They didn't have to come here."

I am moved…I've never seen the Lord like this. I sense He is experiencing distress…and it's something I'm sure I can't experience the same way He does.

"But you can," He says, as He looks up toward me. "You must. If you want to know my heart, you must see and experience this too."

I'm stunned. I don't know what to say.

"And so this will continue, until My Church takes up what I have given them and do battle in My name."

I am left with this picture and continue to see human spirits falling into the cauldron below...

Reflections afterwards...
I'm stunned. This took me by complete surprise. There is a lot to think about. I never expected to see *anything* like this. I am well aware of scriptural references that describe such a scenario. I knew I was seeing souls of the condemned falling into what they would experience for eternity.

I am reminded of 2 Peter 3:9, "The Lord...does not want anyone to perish." Jesus reaffirmed this, *"This is not what I intended." "I did not want this to happen."*

A question the scriptures do not address as clearly as some might wish: What about those who've never had the opportunity to hear the gospel and make a choice? However, the scriptures are *abundantly* clear about those who *have* heard and chosen. Those who choose to believe and trust in Jesus will receive eternal life. Those who willfully choose to reject Him, will face eternal judgement.

While witnessing the horrible fate of the souls in this vision, I had a very strong sense these were those who willfully rejected God's offer. Jesus confirmed and reinforced this, *"They have made their choice... They have done this to themselves... They would not listen!"*

It was so shocking; there were so many of them.

When I saw the Lord in distress, I knew this had to really affect Him. After all, He died for these people too. They willfully rejected the free gift He offered them. In essence, it's as if they slapped the One who loved them in the face and said, "Go away!! We don't want you!!"

I couldn't imagine possibly feeling and understanding this the way Jesus did. After all, He died for these people. However, knowing my thoughts, He then dropped this bomb saying, *"But you can... You must. If you want to know my heart, you must see and experience this too."*

Initially this sent me reeling...but I knew it was true. Something I've been seeking in recent times with greater fervor is to know the Lord's heart—to have a compassion for people that mirrors His compassion. Some years ago, I went on my first mission trip to South America with Gary Oates and ministered to a great many people. I had a concern for those I ministered to, but a *burning compassion?* A compassion like the Lords? No. And I was aware of that. I was in part, still wrapped up in my own issues which inhibited me from reaching out with full effectiveness.

But the Holy Spirit was gently working with me and brought this to my attention. I knew there were still stony areas in my heart that needed renewal, so I continued to seek Him. *I was not content to remain the way I was.*

Fast-forward six years to another trip with Gary to South America. One of my goals when ministering during that trip was to see people more as the Lord does. It turns out, the Holy Spirit had performed a work in me to a depth I hadn't even realized. I witnessed in myself a new compassion for people unlike anything I had previously known. People would come with various problems and diseases wanting to be healed—and my heart went out to them. I found myself hating how the enemy had been torturing these people. I was so overwhelmed with compassion, I found it hard not to just weep over them. With only a few exceptions, nearly everyone I prayed for on that trip was healed! Two different men, both nearly blind in one eye had their vision restored. A lady with a bad leg, bad arm and two lumps—one in each breast—was completely healed. Another young man had a tumor on his hip that shrunk and vanished. Isn't the Lord wonderful?

However, this latest vision addressed something that was still missing — a *burning* compassion for the lost. Was I concerned? Yes. But did I have a *burning* compassion like the Lord's? No. Having a burning compassion puts our hearts 100% in step with the Lord's. And that's when He can really use us. In the last few days since experiencing this vision, I've had some additional "mini visions," so to speak, where I've experienced an increasing sensitivity to the Lord's heart in this vital area.

So, my adventure — the quest to have my heart totally submitted and mirror the Lord's heart continues...

And then there was the last thing the Lord said... "And so this will continue, until My Church takes up what I have given them and do battle in My name."

A person could write *volumes* on everything potentially contained within that one sentence...

- He's given us His Holy Spirit.
- He's given us the fruits of the Spirit.
- He's given us the gifts of the Spirit.
- He's given us His Word.
- And He's given us a commission.

But what has the church done with these? Many in the church have set aside some of what the Lord has given us. How then can we effectively carry out the commission He also gave us?

Some have set aside the power of the Holy Spirit, teaching the Lord no longer works that way. Some have set aside the fruits of the Spirit leading to moral bankruptcy and the collapse of ministries. In worst case scenarios, some have even set aside God's Word, claiming it to be just a collection of nice, or even irrelevant stories. Is it any wonder the church at large has been so ineffective — for centuries — bringing multitudes the Lord?

There is indeed *a lot* packed into that last statement from the Lord. I'm sure I will continue to meditate on this...

In a completely different realm — as often happens, my rational mind is quick to step to the front and ask questions; where was this? In the earlier vision I referred to, the Lord definitely identified that place as the abyss. However, He didn't identify this place, nor did I ask. He did say previously; I would visit the abyss with Him again. However, are human spirits thrown into the abyss?

I did an online study and found a lengthy article where the author discusses and compares places like the abyss, hades, hell, and the "lake of fire." Although well studied, I felt the author was quick to make a sizable number of definitive conclusions about these places. Despite the author's assertions to the contrary, the Bible does not actually provide a great deal of *definitive* information about these locations. In fact, the author resorted to gleaning information from questionable, non-canonical sources (such as the book of Enoch) in order to support his conclusions.

As often happens in Biblical studies, some tend to overly pontificate on subjects we actually know little about. Therefore, in my opinion, we should be very careful making rigid, definitive conclusions.

The fact is, knowing precisely where this occurred is probably not important. Had it been vital, I'm sure the Lord would have said something. What I can say is this — it was a place of torment and human spirits were being cast into it. And the Bible repeatedly confirms such a place exists. In Luke chapter 16, Jesus himself mentions hades...and that it is a place of torment for the unrepentant. I suspect the abyss and hades are somehow related, as their descriptions in the scriptures are very similar. Perhaps the abyss is located within Hades? I don't think anyone can truly say with certainty.

However, the important thing about this vision was not *where* it was happening, but the fact it *was* happening — and the Lord wanted me to see it. There is no question seeing this has changed me and continues to do so. If we wish to know God intimately, we must know His heart. His heart is the core of who He is. To know His heart is to know Him.

I'm thankful for the Lord's faithfulness as He continues to work in my heart, slowly bringing it into conformity with His own. My desire is to continue yielding myself and allowing Him to do His work. Sometimes the process is unpleasant. However, it's not all unpleasant...sometimes the experience is wonderful as the Lord brings new revelation and healing.

Looking back over all this, I'm particularly thankful I've been consciously aware — on many occasions — my heart was lacking and not mirroring the Lord's. Rather than ignoring this awareness, I chose to seek the Lord and pleaded with Him to fill in that which was lacking. I might add this was not a one-time occurrence. Rather this process...and my pursuit has taken years.

I consider the awareness I had a gift from God. Without it, I wouldn't be in a position to choose, act and pursue change. But as Jesus taught us, isn't this the job of the Holy Spirit? He speaks...and brings us into all truth! Amen!

Conclusions from This Journey So Far

As mentioned at the beginning of part two, the last several years of my life have been tumultuous. After living and working in the UK for nearly 10 years, the Lord engineered circumstances—and did so very quickly—leading me back to Florida, where I previously lived. Periods of tumult and uncertainly began a few years before leaving the UK and continued after my return to the States. There were clouds of uncertainty surrounding both employment and housing. Numerous, significant, unexpected expenses were dumped into my path. However, through it all, the Lord has provided.

Interestingly, the experiences recorded in this book began at about the same time all the tumult began. I cannot begin to emphasize how encouraging and valuable these encounters have been. There is no question the Lord used these to help anchor me in place during the ensuing storms. From a practical point of view, they've helped in several specific ways:

- First, the Lord used a few experiences to warn me of difficult times ahead...and the need to trust Him through it all. Lessons in trust have been a frequent theme.

- Secondly, the encounters helped ground me in the Lord in new, powerful, experiential ways. For example, it's one thing to read about the Lord providing help to someone in times of need. It's quite another to experience it firsthand. As such, these experiences provided strength and encouragement in ways that were very real and impactful. The full impact did not always manifest immediately. However, as I meditated on the experiences, many would take on even richer meaning and sink deeper into my spirit.

- Thirdly, there are aspects of the Lord's personality, His love and affection for me that have become a reality within my soul and spirit beyond anything I had ever previously experienced. In other words, I have come to "know" Him better. And that was the number one reason

I was seeking Him in the first place!! (And I must add, that process is *far* from over!)

At certain times, the visions have become less frequent, in part because of all the turmoil and distractions around me. (I'm still learning to cope with that.) However, something else has been happening as well. I've also been devoting more time meditating on what I already experienced. I found (and still find) myself rereading previous encounters and discovering more and more substance in them. I continue to see and understand new things. Even individual phrases sometimes leap out at me with a fresh and new impact. (The Lord told me this would happen…but it's something to actually experience it.)

Even after several years of encounters, I still feel I have only just barely scratched the surface of experiencing what He desires to share.

In conclusion, I repeat what I said in the first chapter: The Lord wants to speak to every one of us. I'm no different from anybody else. If I can hear God speak and have encounters with Him, anybody can. Therefore, I hope this encourages others to seek and pursue the Lord with all their heart, soul and mind.

— APPENDEX —

The Most Important Key to Entering and Experiencing the Spiritual Realm

I never went into these experiences desiring to see angels, or for that matter, anything else in the spiritual realm. No. I was pursuing a more intimate relationship with the Lord…period. As my experiences testified, they sometimes included angelic encounters and seeing heavenly places, but these were all experienced as God orchestrated them…*not according to my own desires.*

I cannot end this book without clearly stating the following truths. Many today are desirous of having angelic encounters, having spiritual experiences and entering the unseen spiritual realm. However, this path is fraught with potential danger. Jesus clearly said, *"Enter through the narrow gate. For wide is the gate and broad is the road that leads to destruction, and many enter through it. But small is the gate and narrow the road that leads to life, and only a few find it."* — Matthew 7:13,14

So, what is the narrow gate? And what is the "broad road" leading to destruction? Jesus said:

*"**I am the gate**; whoever enters through me will be saved."* — John 10:9

Jesus is the one and only safe way God has provided for us. Jesus reiterated this many times. *"**I am the way** and the truth and the life. **No one comes to the Father except through me**."* — John 14:6

He didn't mince words. Jesus said *He is the way*. He is the truth. He is the life. And *no one can come to God except through Him*. Many today teach, or wish to believe, there are many spiritual paths to God. But Jesus *clearly and explicitly* refuted that.

So then, what is the "broad road" that leads to destruction? The answer is simple—everything and everyone who claims they offer an alternate route into the spiritual realm to God. Jesus specifically said of them, *"At that time if anyone says to you, 'Look, here is the Messiah!' or, 'There he is!' do not believe it. For false messiahs and false prophets will appear…"* — Matthew 24:23

Techniques such as emptying one's mind, repetitive reciting of special prayers or mantras, attempts to gain access with physical objects like crystals, manipulating one's mind with drugs, or soliciting "spiritual guides," are all part of the "broad road" to destruction. The scriptures warn us, *"There is a way that appears to be right, but in the end it leads to death."* —Proverbs 16:25

Jesus made it clear, He alone is the "narrow gate." He repeatedly proved this. The apostle Peter said in Acts 2:22, *"Jesus of Nazareth was a man accredited by God to you by miracles, wonders and signs, which God did among you through him…"* To which Paul added, *"He has given proof of this to everyone by raising him from the dead."* —Acts 17:31

No man—no prophet in history accomplished what Jesus did. He quite literally proved Himself…and proved what He said was true.

Therefore, the most important key to experiencing the spiritual realm is personally knowing Jesus Christ. It's not simply knowing *about* Him—but having an intimate relationship with Him. Perhaps the best example is the relationship between husband and wife. They don't just *know about* each other. Rather, from their life experiences together, they know each other *intimately*; thoroughly. That is the kind of experience Jesus desires to have with us.

Some have taught that we must somehow earn our way into heaven by performing good works, saying lots of prayers and attending church regularly. However, Jesus sets the record straight regarding that:

"[The disciples] asked him, 'What must we do to do the works God requires?' Jesus answered, 'The work of God is this: to believe in the one he has sent.'" —John 6:28,29

Notice the disciples asked what "works" God required. The common thought at the time was, one had to perform a series of works—do them a certain way—and complete a list of tasks to earn favour with God. However, Jesus didn't respond with a list of works (plural), but responded with the singular, "work." *"The work of God is: to believe in the one he has sent."* Very simply, getting connected with God requires believing Jesus is who He said He was…the one and only gate to God…and believing what He taught. But the word "believe" in the original languages means more than head knowledge. The kind of belief the scriptures refer to is something that comes from the heart — it's more than simply acknowledging facts with our heads. It's also *experiencing* Him.

So how do we connect with Jesus? Simple! We invite Him with an open heart! But to do that, there are a few things we need to understand.

From the very beginning, God desired to have a personal, intimate relationship with mankind. Our original forbearers, Adam and Eve, had an incredible relationship with God. But regretfully, they were deceived. Instead of choosing God's road, they chose their own road…the easy, broad road. It "seemed right" to them, but in reality, led to destruction. That bad choice and the fallout it created, poisoned the minds of all who followed.

The deliberate violation of God's instructions resulted in catastrophe. God is absolutely pure and holy. Adam and Eve's violation…the Bible calls it sin…disrupted the intimate relationship they enjoyed with God. Sin cannot stand in the presence of a holy God. With that intimate relationship severed, Adam, Eve and their decedents plunged into a downward spiral towards further rebellion and wickedness.

This created a dilemma for God. He deeply loved mankind…and wanted that intimate fellowship back — He longed for His creation. The problem was, God being perfectly righteous and holy, cannot tolerate sin in His presence. The two are simply incompatible. Being perfectly holy is one of God's attributes, but the scriptures also tell us God is perfectly just. *"He will by no means leave the guilty unpunished."* — Exodus 34:7 NASB

So, perfect justice required mankind's rebellion be punished. Because sin could not exist before a holy God, the only possible punishment was severing the relationship — forever. This is spiritual death…eternal separation from God.

However, God devised an ingenious plan to see justice was

served and give mankind a chance to return to Him. His plan was prefigured in ancient Israel. *A substitution would take place.* On a regular basis, animals were sacrificed for the sins of the people. So, punishment was poured out, but on innocent animals instead of the people. But this was merely a picture of the final solution. Since the original rebellion started with a man, the final, permanent solution required punishment to be poured out onto a man.

God's plan was hatched. Jesus, who existed eternally as one with His Father, was to strip Himself of His rights to remain alongside His Father...and come to earth as a man. He came for the sole purpose of offering Himself as THE human sacrifice for the totality of mankind's sin, imperfection and failure:

"Christ Jesus: Who, being in very nature God, did not consider equality with God something to be used to his own advantage; rather, he made himself nothing by taking the very nature of a servant, being made in human likeness. And being found in appearance as a man, he humbled himself by becoming obedient to death — even death on a cross!" —Philippians 2:6-8

So, two thousand years ago, Jesus came and took the punishment that mankind deserved. The punishment was death. But after that punishment was poured out and the penalty paid, something remarkable happened.

God wanted to demonstrate an amazing gift He was going to offer mankind. To demonstrate that gift, God the Father raised Jesus from the dead! This was to foreshadow the gift God is now offering to us all.

You see, each of us with our imperfections, are as good as dead, *"For all have sinned and fall short of the glory of God."* —Romans 3:23

But just as God raised Jesus from the dead, He now offers to "raise us from the dead" as well! What does this mean? It means we can have incredible fellowship with God restored *right now*...and it will last for eternity!

Best of all, it's a free gift, because Jesus paid the penalty: *"For the wages of sin is death, but the gift of God is eternal life in Christ Jesus our Lord."* —Romans 6:23

The apostle Paul confirms this again…and hints how this gift is received: *"For it is by grace you have been saved,* **through faith** *— and this is not from yourselves, it is* **the gift of God**" — Ephesians 2:8

However, like any gift, we need to willfully receive it. God doesn't force it on us. Here's an illustration: Suppose I'm standing in front of you with my hand out. Laying on the palm of my hand is a ten-dollar bill. I extend it towards you and say, "Here, this is free. It's yours." What happens next depends how you respond. If you stand there and do nothing, the money will continue to just sit there unclaimed. However, if you willfully reach out, take and *receive it,* you now possess it! As the giver, I already did what I could. To actually possess the gift, you must willfully reach out and receive it.

The same is true with the gift of eternal life God offers us. Jesus has already paid the price for all our mistakes, faults and yes, deliberate sin. By doing so, He purchased the gift of life which He now freely offers us. Just like the 10-dollar bill in my hand, Jesus offers us the gift of intimate fellowship and eternal life, if we are willing to accept it. So, how do we do that?

In the book of Acts, someone asked the apostle Paul and his friend Silas that very question: *"Sirs, what must I do to be saved?" They replied, "Believe in the Lord Jesus, and you will be saved…"*
Acts 16:30,31

So, what does it mean to believe? As mentioned earlier, in the original languages, believing implies more than having simple head knowledge. It is something active; *it is trusting Jesus completely.* It involves making a decision. It means turning away from our own efforts (which will always be inadequate) and accepting (putting our faith in) what Jesus Christ has already done for us.

So, to receive this gift from Jesus, all we need to do is to ask Him — with a humble heart. And He promises this: *"I won't send away anyone who comes to me."* — John 6:37 CEB

You can offer up a simple prayer like the following:

"Lord, I'm sorry for the things I've done in my life that weren't pleasing to You. I willfully turn away from them...and turn to You. I trust You with my life and give it into Your hands. You said You would never turn away anyone who comes to You. I now trust You with that promise. I believe You are the Son of God, and ask for the gift of eternal life you purchased for me."

If you honestly offered that prayer from your heart, the Lord will answer it...in fact He has already done so, and you have become a child of God!

"Yet to all who did receive him, to those who believed in his name, he gave the right to become children of God." —John 1:12

I would encourage you to find a good bible believing church to attend — one that believes God can still speak to us today and performs miracles. God uses good Christian fellowship to help us along in our pursuit of knowing Him.

A final note: God, through Jesus, is the ultimate source of all knowledge. Therefore, our focus must be resolutely fixed on Jesus and no one else. The apostle Paul refers to Jesus, *"in whom are hidden all the treasures of wisdom and knowledge."* —Colossians 2:3

Think of it! All of God's treasures of wisdom and knowledge are in Jesus! This means to really know God, *we must know Jesus.* The best way to begin knowing Him is to start reading His Word as contained in the Bible. The gospel of John is a good place to start. Within it, one can witness the heart of Jesus in action...what He's really like is revealed.

"Therefore, everyone who hears these words of mine and puts them into practice is like a wise man who built his house on the rock. The rain came down, the streams rose, and the winds blew and beat against that house; yet it did not fall, because it had its foundation on the rock. But everyone who hears these words of mine and does not put them into practice is like a foolish man who built his house on sand. The rain came down, the streams rose, and the winds blew and beat against that house, and it fell with a great crash." Matthew 7:24-27

A final prayer from my own heart…

"Lord Jesus, I just ask that you bless every person who has made the decision to follow You. May Your Holy Spirit guide them as they read Your word…and guide them into an intimate knowledge of You. In Your name I ask this…Amen."

Suggested Reading

Open My Eyes, Lord
By Gary Oates
www.garyoates.com

As mentioned in the first chapter, it was Gary's testimony and teaching that further quickened my desire to know God more intimately. Although his testimonies are amazing, the teachings are the most important part the book. Gary points out that many today are busy seeking experiences, gifts or more spiritual power. However, that's putting the cart before the horse. Our number one priority should be seeking an *increasingly* intimate relationship with Lord. Everything else flows naturally out of that relationship. Part of Gary's unique presentation is how he sanctifies his senses for the Lord's use. With God's blessings, our spiritual eyes, ears and other senses can then be opened to perceive things in the spiritual realm...leading to even more intimate experiences with the Lord.

How to Hear God's Voice
By Mark & Patti Virkler
www.cwgministries.org

Gary Oates' teachings laid the initial foundation. Then the Virkler's book, "How to Hear God's Voice" was like turning an ignition key that really propelled me forward. For years Mark and Patti have taught a course on this subject. The book is a 300-page manual for that course. It is the most in-depth treatment on the subject of hearing God's voice I've ever encountered. Many hundreds of scriptures are provided in this context. The Virklers not only directly address this subject, but just as importantly address many crucial, related topics on the subject of prayer, quieting ourselves before the Lord and the need for discernment. As such, this book addresses the subject in the widest possible scope.

I spent a couple months digesting this material. If a person is truly interested in pursuing God with all their heart...and desire to clearly hear Him, this book is a fabulous resource. Highly recommended.

When Heaven Touches Earth
By Gary Greig, James Goll, Mark Virkler, Mike Rogers, Maurice Fuller
Available from www.cwgministries.org

A pre-release version of this book was given to me by one of the authors, Mike Rogers. Receiving it was an amazing example of God's timing and provision. It was exactly what I needed at the moment. I had several experiences that were of such a nature, I initially questioned their legitimacy — even though they were highly encouraging and I had a sense of the Lord's presence throughout. This book addresses the Biblical validity of such experiences in a series of papers written by the above authors. It presents compelling evidence that God is by no means silent today! Furthermore, He may choose to speak in ways that can truly surprise us!

The Coming Shift
By Larry Randolph
www.larryrandolph.com

Though Larry Randolph is a leading prophetic figure, this book does not deal directly with the subject of journaling and personal prophecy. Rather, it deals with something far more fundamental and crucial if we hope to maintain a dialog with the Lord...and continue hearing Him clearly. It deals with our willingness to accept change, both in ourselves and within the church at large. If the Lord reveals things to us, but we refuse to act on them, there's little reason for Him to continue speaking. However, if we are willing to embrace what He says — which can involve changing how we think — He will know we are serious about pushing further into the things of Him and reward us accordingly. I can't imagine anyone reading this book without being challenged in some facet of their Christian walk. Highly recommended.

About the Author

In the secular realm, Doug Tews has held the same job for over 40 years. He has what must be one of the rarest jobs on earth: Creating programs for synchronized water, light and music displays. Samples of his unusual, creative work can be seen on his YouTube channel: Douglas Tews

Doug was born and raised in a suburb of Milwaukee, Wisconsin. As a child, he was baptized and confirmed in the Lutheran church. He came to a personal knowledge of the Lord Jesus Christ while in college through Baptist friends and the ministry of the Navigators.

After transferring to a different college, he continued to forge friendships across denominational lines through Intervarsity Christian Fellowship. His life was then deeply impacted in the 1970's through the ministry of a group of charismatic Catholics and Lutherans.

After graduating from college, the Lord opened doors for Doug to move to south Florida, where he was a member of the Wesleyan church for many years.

In late 2005, Doug's work took him to the Isle of Wight in the UK where he lived for nearly ten years. It became apparent, the Lord was doing a significant work there, which Doug was pleased to be a part of. In 2015, the Lord engineered circumstances bringing him back to Florida, where he resides today.

Through the years, Doug's relationship with God has been fully Christ centered, not denominationally centered. His eclectic Christian experience across denominational lines allows him to freely communicate and relate to Christians of all backgrounds.

Today, Doug enjoys speaking to people, exhorting them in the knowledge, God has *far more* for people to experience in Him than they ever imagined. His book is a living example of that.

Doug Tews may be contacted at:
welcome@meetingjesus.net

Made in the USA
Columbia, SC
03 March 2022